M1994
.W313M32
1970

02118 00075 5829 6285 $4.00 81120

Book Three

The Magic of Music

LORRAIN E. WATTERS / LOUIS G. WERSEN / WILLIAM C. HARTSHORN

L. EILEEN McMILLAN / ALICE GALLUP / FREDERICK BECKMAN

Illustrations by Robert DeCoste, Walt Disney Productions, J. P. Miller, and Leonard Weisgard

GINN AND COMPANY

A XEROX COMPANY

© Copyright, 1970, 1966, by Ginn and Company All Rights Reserved

Home Office, Boston, Massachusetts 02117

Library of Congress Catalog Card Number: 65–1603

Acknowledgments

The Association for Childhood Education International and Lillian Schulz Vanada, for "Fuzzy Wuzzy, Creepy Crawly," from *Sung Under the Silver Umbrella*, Copyright 1935. The Macmillan Company, New York, N.Y. By permission of the Association for Childhood Education International, Washington, D.C.

Beacon Press, for "Lovely Secret Gardens Grow" ("Secret Gardens") (melody) and "Today the Sky Is Very Far Away," from *We Sing of Life*, published by Starr King Press, reprinted by permission of the Beacon Press, copyright 1955 by The American Ethical Union.

The Boy Scouts Association, for "We're All Together Again," from *Boy Scout Songbook of England*.

Cooperative Recreation Service, Inc., for "Four in a Boat," from *Handy Play Party Book*, copyright 1940 by Lynn Rohrbough, and for "Little Johnny England," from *Chansons de Notre Chalet*, copyright 1957, 1959, 1962 by Cooperative Recreation Service, Inc.

Cooperative Recreation Service, Inc. and J. D. Elder, for "There Was a Little Sandy Girl" ("Sandy Girl"), from *Song-Games of Trinidad and Tobago*, copyright 1961 by Cooperative Recreation Service, Inc.

E. P. Dutton & Co., Inc., for "Thanksgiving" (excerpt), copyright, 1941, by Marchette Chute. From the book *Around and About* by Marchette Chute. Published 1957 by E. P. Dutton & Co., Inc. and reprinted with their permission.

Aileen Fisher, for "Down in the Hollow" (excerpt).

Friendship Press, for "Praise and Thanksgiving" (words), translated and paraphrased by Edith Lovell Thomas, from *The Whole World Singing* by Edith Lovell Thomas, © 1950, Friendship Press, Inc., New York, New York.

Ginn and Company, for "We Thank Thee," from *Songs of Childhood*, copyright 1923, of the Music Education Series. For "Things I Like Best," from *Rhythms and Rimes*, copyright 1936, 1943, and for "O Jesu Sweet," from *On Wings of Song*, copyright 1945, 1949, of The World of Music series. For "I Can Play and Sing," from *Singing on Our Way*, copyright 1949, 1957, 1959, and for "The Friendly Beasts," "Night Herding Song," "Oh, Poor Chick-a-biddy," "Out on the Ocean," and "Three Pirates," from *Singing Every Day*, copyright 1950, 1957, 1959, of Our Singing World series. For "Sing, Sing Along" and "Snow-White Little Burro," from *We Sing and Dance*, copyright 1957, of We Sing and Praise series. For "Dance-A-Story about Balloons," © 1964. And for "The Call of the Ocean," from *Ginn Music News*, © 1965.

Harcourt, Brace & World, Inc., for "Hallowe'en," from *The Little Hill*, copyright, 1949, by Harry Behn. Reprinted by permission of Harcourt, Brace & World, Inc.

Mildred P. Harrington, for "Lullaby" ("Sleep") (words) and "My Little Boat" (excerpt), from *Ring-A-Round*, by Mildred P. Harrington, copyright 1930 by The Macmillan Company.

Holt, Rinehart and Winston, Inc., for "Theme in Yellow," from *Chicago Poems* by Carl Sandburg. Copyright 1916 by Holt, Rinehart and Winston, Inc. Copyright 1944 by Carl Sandburg. Reprinted by permission of Holt, Rinehart and Winston, Inc.

J. B. Lippincott Company, for "Outside the Door," from *For Days and Days* by Annette Wynne. Copyright 1919, 1947 by Annette Wynne. Published by J. B. Lippincott Company.

Little, Brown and Company and David McCord, for "The Rainbow" (excerpt), from *Far and Few* by David McCord, by permission of the author and Little, Brown and Company.

The Macmillan Company, for "Morning and Afternoon" (words), from *Poems*, by Elizabeth J. Coatsworth, copyright 1934 by The Macmillan Company; for "The White Window" ("The Quiet Moon") (words), from *Collected Poems*, by James Stephens, copyright 1935 by The Macmillan Company; and for "Woods' Litany," from *Country Poems*, by Elizabeth Coatsworth.

Mrs. Ilo Orleans, for "The Singers," from *I Watch the World Go By*, by Ilo Orleans, published by Henry Z. Walck, Inc., by permission of Mrs. Ilo Orleans.

Oxford University Press, for "Children's Song of the Nativity" ("How Far Is It to Bethlehem?") (melody) and "Rocking," from *The Oxford Book of Carols*, and for "Praise to the Lord" (words), from *The English Hymnal*, by permission of Oxford University Press.

Laurence Pollinger Limited, for "Theme in Yellow," from *Chicago Poems* by Carl Sandburg, published by Jonathan Cape Limited, and Holt, Rinehart and Winston, Inc., proprietors.

Alan Swallow, for "Little Day Moon" (words), from *The Sun Drops Red*, by Nellie Burget Miller, published by Sage Books, Inc.

Teachers Publishing Corporation, for "Know It Is Christmas," by Lois Snelling, from the December 1955 issue of *Grade Teacher*.

Nancy Byrd Turner, for "Easter Joy."

A. P. Watt & Son and Miss D. E. Collins, for "How Far Is It to Bethlehem?" (words), from *The Oxford Book of Carols*.

Wonderland Music Company, Inc., for "Chim Chim Cher-ee," "Feed the Birds," "Let's Go Fly a Kite," "The Perfect Nanny," "A Spoonful of Sugar," "Step in Time," and "Supercalifragilisticexpialidocious," words and music by Richard M. Sherman and Robert B. Sherman © 1963 Wonderland Music Company, Inc.

All illustrations on pages 63 through 70, 73, 74, and 76 through 80 © Walt Disney Productions.

In the case of some material for which acknowledgment is not given, we have earnestly endeavored to find the original source and to procure permission for its use, but without success.

Contents

There's Magic in Music

There's magic in singing. . . .

How Do You Do Today?

Carol Davis

Italian Folk Melody

Allegro

Bright and ear - ly in the morn - ing

When you go a - long your way,

Hap - py smiles will sure - ly greet you

If to ev - 'ry-one you say:

6

"Oh, how do you do to-day?

Oh, how do you do to-day?

Oh, how do you do to-day, my friend,

Oh, how do you do to-day?"

There's magic in listening. . . .

Children's Prayer

Translated

From *Hansel and Gretel*
Engelbert Humperdinck

Andante

When at night I go to sleep, Four-teen an-gels watch do—keep;

Two are here a-bove me, Two are there be-low—— me,

Two are by my right hand, Two are by my left hand,

Two who warm-ly cov-er, Two who warm-ly hov-er,

Two who take me when I rise, And lead my steps to Par-a-dise.

Humperdinck wrote music for the story of *Hansel and Gretel*.

For Listening: Prelude to *Hansel and Gretel* — Humperdinck
(RCA Victor, ADVENTURES IN MUSIC, Grade 5, Vol. 2)

There's magic in playing instruments. . . .

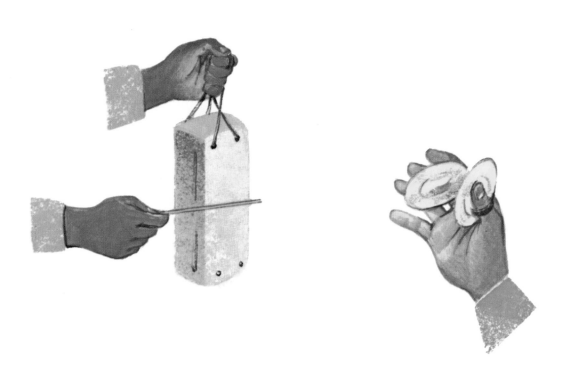

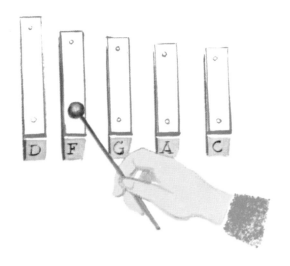

After School

Grace Boynton

Chinese Folk Melody

Andante

School is__ out as the sun goes down;

Books in my bag I go through the town.

Home are my par - ents who smile at me;

I make a nice low bow like this, you see.

For an oriental sound, keep the mallet from bouncing when you strike each tone on the resonator bells.

Play this two-measure pattern throughout the song with percussion instruments.

Finger Cymbals
Wood Block

From THE PAGODA, copyright 1946 by the
Cooperative Recreation Service, Inc., Delaware, Ohio.
Used with permission.

There's magic in marching. . . .

Yankee Doodle

Traditional

In marching tempo

1. Yan-kee Doo-dle came to town A-rid-ing on a po-ny,

He stuck a feath-er in his hat And called it mac-a-ro-ni.

REFRAIN

Yan-kee Doo-dle keep it up, Yan-kee Doo-dle Dan-dy,

Mind the mu-sic and the step, And with the girls be hand-y.

2. Fath'r and I went down to camp,
   Along with Captain Goodwin,
   And there we saw the men and boys,
   As thick as hasty pudding. . . .

3. There was Captain Washington,
   Upon a slapping stallion,
   A-giving orders to his men;
   I guess there was a million. . . .

Play a lively rhythm on the drum as you march and sing.

There's magic in dancing. . . .

Rain-Dance Song

M. M.   *In moderate tempo*   Zuñi Indian

1. Come a-gain,   come a-gain,   come,   good rain,
2. Come a-gain,   come a-gain,   come,   good rain,

Fall up-on the moun-tains,   and   on   the   plain.
Wa-ter for the riv-ers,   and   for   the   grain.

Can you make up a rain dance for this song?
Play an accompaniment throughout while you sing and dance.

15

THE SINGERS

One singer is
  A SOLO,
And two are
  A DUET.

Three singers are
  A TRIO,
And four are
  A QUARTET.

And many voices—
  Boys' and girls'—
Low and high
  And higher,

We hear in church
  Or school are called
A CHORUS or
  A CHOIR!

Ilo Orleans

Music We Can Sing and Play

The Beat of Music

We hear the beat when soldiers march.

left   right   left   right

We hear the beat as the clock ticks.

tick   tock   tick   tock

Meter

Some beats are stronger than others.

These beats are grouped in sets of twos. (*Clap*)

These beats are grouped in sets of twos. (*Clap*)

They are written like this:

The meter is $\frac{2}{4}$.

These beats are grouped in sets of threes. (*Clap*)

They are written like this:

The meter is $\frac{3}{4}$.

These beats are grouped in sets of fours. (*Clap*)

They are written like this:

The meter is $\frac{4}{4}$.

Tempo

The beat of music moves at different speeds.

Elephants move at a slow speed.

Slow ♩ ♩ ♩ ♩

Squirrels scamper about quickly.

Fast ♩ ♩ ♩ ♩

The quarter notes in the first example move at a different speed, or tempo, than the quarter notes in the second example.

A composer can give us the speed at which he feels his music should go by using Italian words such as:

Largo . . . (pronounced *lahr'-goh*) . . . . . . very slow
Adagio . . (pronounced *uh-dah'-joh*) . . . . . slow
Andante . (pronounced *ahn-dahn'-tay*) . . . moderately slow
Moderato . (pronounced *moh-day-rah'-toh*) . moderate tempo
Allegretto . (pronounced *ahl-lay-greht'-toh*) . moderately fast
Allegro . . (pronounced *ahl-lay'-groh*) . . . . fast
Presto . . . (pronounced *preh'-stoh*) . . . . . very fast

A composer can also give us the speed by indicating a metronome mark. In an automobile we have a speedometer that tells us the speed at which we travel. In music we have a metronome that tells us the speed or tempo of the music.

SPEEDOMETER

METRONOME

21

This melody has five different tones.
The home tone (1, or *do*) is C.

I Can Play and Sing

Susan Anthony

Slowly

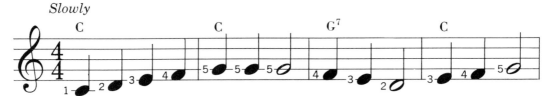

I   can play a   lit - tle tune, Lit - tle tune,   lit - tle tune;

When I play I   sing a song   All the day   long.

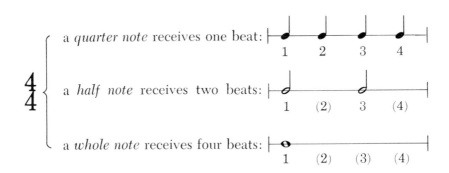

a *quarter note* receives one beat:

        1 2 3 4

a *half note* receives two beats:

        1 (2) 3 (4)

a *whole note* receives four beats:

        1 (2) (3) (4)

How many different tones are there in this melody?

Lovely Evening

Traditional Round

Rather slowly

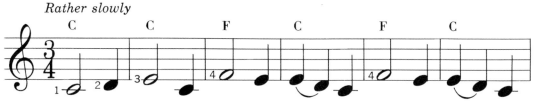

Oh, how love - ly is the eve - ning, is the eve - ning,

When the bells are sweet-ly ring - ing, sweet-ly ring - ing!

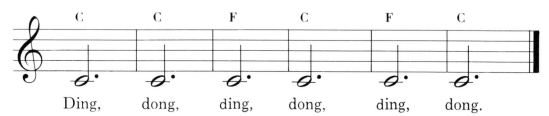

Ding,   dong,   ding,   dong,   ding,   dong.

$\dfrac{3}{4}$ {
a quarter note (♩) receives one beat.
a half note (♪) receives two beats.
a *dotted half note* (♩.) receives three beats.
}

Charles Gounod, a great composer, wrote this beautiful music for a chorus and orchestra. Make it sound as beautiful as you can.

Lovely Appear

Translated by J. Troutbeck

From *The Redemption*
Charles Gounod

Love - ly ap - pear o - ver the moun - tains,

The feet of them that preach, and bring good news of peace,

The feet of them that preach, and bring good news of peace.

This sign is a *quarter rest*: 𝄽

The quarter rest tells you to be silent for one beat in this song.

What is the name of the home tone?
Does the melody end on the home tone?

Snow-White Little Burro

S. C.

Chilean Folk Melody

Moderately fast

1. Snow-white lit - tle   bur - ro,   Take me   for   a   ride
2. Sad - dle bells are   jin - gling   As   you   trot   a - long.

Down the rock - y   val - ley,   Up   the   moun-tain - side.
You   will play the   mu - sic,   I   will   sing   a   song.

Say the words and tap the rhythm of the melody in measures one and two.

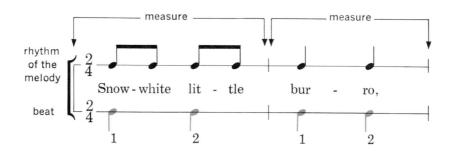

rhythm of the melody

Snow - white   lit - tle   bur - ro,

beat   1   2   1   2

How many notes are in the first measure?
How many beats are in the first measure?

These notes are *eighth notes*:
There are two eighth notes for each beat.

25

This is a *staff*:

This is a *treble clef* on the staff: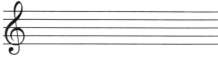

The short line below the staff is called a *ledger line*.

This is a *scale* going up:

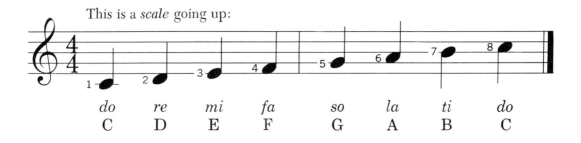

do	re	mi	fa	so	la	ti	do
C	D	E	F	G	A	B	C

This is a *scale* going down:

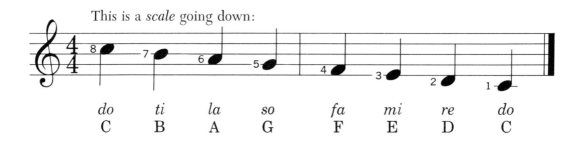

do	ti	la	so	fa	mi	re	do
C	B	A	G	F	E	D	C

Notes may have three kinds of names: { numeral, syllable, letter }

Sing the C major scale with numerals, then with letters.
Are all the tones of the scale used in this melody?

How many different kinds of notes do you see?

Little Dove

K. S.

Smoothly

Czech Folk Melody

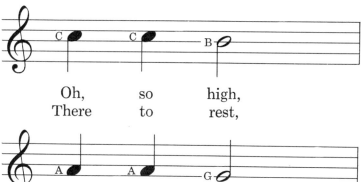

C - D - E - F - G - A - B - G

1. O - ver - head   a   dove was fly - ing,
2. Do you have   a   home at night-time,

C   C   B

Oh,   so   high,
There   to   rest,

A   A   G

In   the   sky.
In   the   nest?

F - A - F - D - E - G - E - C - D - D - C

Lit - tle dove, so far a - bove, Where do   you   fly?
Lit - tle dove, so far a - bove, Then you   are   blest.

C D E F G A B C   do re mi fa so la ti do   1 2 3 4 5 6 7 8

27

This song is in the *key* of C major.
The home tone (1, or *do*) is C.

French Cradle Song

Translated by J. T. W.

French Folk Song

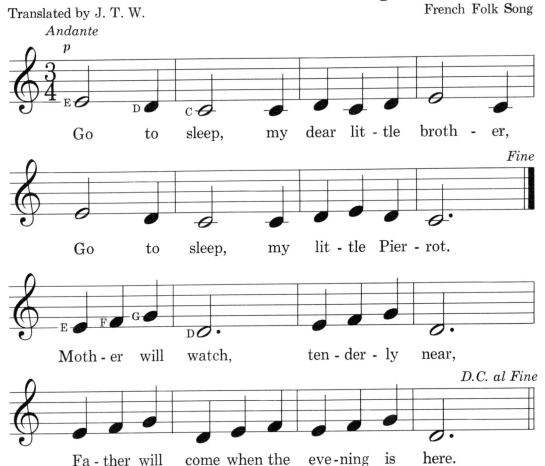

Andante

p

Go to sleep, my dear lit - tle broth - er,

Fine

Go to sleep, my lit - tle Pier - rot.

Moth - er will watch, ten - der - ly near,

D.C. al Fine

Fa - ther will come when the eve - ning is here.

D.C. al Fine means to go back to the beginning and sing to the
word *Fine* (pronounced *fee-nay*) where the song ends.

You can play and sing a song in many keys.
Now the *key* is F major and the home tone is F.
The melody is the same but it looks higher on the staff.
It also sounds higher.

French Cradle Song

Translated by J. T. W.   French Folk Song

Go to sleep, my dear lit-tle broth-er,

Go to sleep, my lit-tle Pier-rot.

Moth-er will watch, ten-der-ly near,

Fa-ther will come when the eve-ning is here.

Sing the melody with syllables in the key of C major.

29

The musical ideas which make up songs are called *phrases*.

Each line of this song is a musical phrase.

Try to sing each phrase with one breath.

We Thank Thee

Elizabeth Taylor

Traditional Hymn Melody

1. Fa - ther, we thank Thee for sun - shine so bright;
2. Fa - ther, we thank Thee for friends kind and true;

Thy lov - ing care that pro - tects us by night;
May we be faith - ful in all that we do.

For par - ents dear, for work and play,
Oh, let us sing, and let us say,

Fa - ther, we thank Thee, day af - ter day.
"Fa - ther, we thank Thee, day af - ter day."

This is a *flat*: ♭

A flat lowers the pitch of a tone a half step.

Find B♭ on the bells or on the piano.

All Through the Night

Sir Harold Boulton

Welsh Folk Melody

Andante

Sleep, my child, and peace at-tend thee All through the night;

Guard-ian an-gels God will send thee All through the night.

Soft the drow-sy hours are creep-ing,

Hill and vale in slum-ber steep-ing,

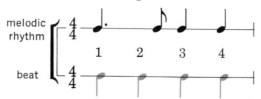

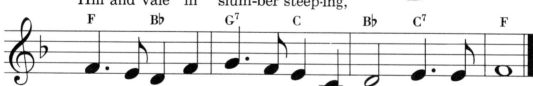

I my lov-ing vig-il keep-ing All through the night.

The first note is a *dotted quarter note.*
A dot increases the duration of a note by one-half.

The second note is an *eighth note.*
Its value is one-half of a quarter note.

melodic rhythm

1 2 3 4

beat

This beautiful song of praise has been sung for many years in many lands.

Praise to the Lord

Joachim Neander
Translated by Catherine Winkworth

Traditional German Hymn

Allegro

Praise to the Lord, the Al-might-y, the King of cre - a - tion!

O my soul, praise Him, for He is thy health and sal - va - tion!

All ye who hear, Now to His tem - ple draw near;

Join me in glad ad - o - ra - tion.

There is one flat in the key of F major.

What is the letter name of the home tone?

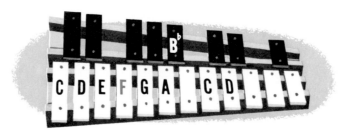

Now the *key* is G major and the home tone is G.
The melody is the same but it looks higher on the staff.
It also sounds higher.

Praise to the Lord

Joachim Neander
Translated by Catherine Winkworth

Traditional German **Hymn**

Praise to the Lord, the Al-might-y, the King of cre - a - tion!

O my soul, praise Him, for He is thy health and sal - va - tion!

All ye who hear, Now to His tem - ple draw near;

Join me in glad ad - o - ra - tion.

This is a *sharp*: ♯
A sharp raises the pitch of a tone a half step.
Find F♯ on the bells or on the piano.

33

The great musician Ludwig van Beethoven composed this melody as an important part of his famous Ninth Symphony.

Ode to Joy

Friedrich von Schiller
Adapted

Ludwig van Beethoven

Sing we now in joy and glad - ness

O'er the earth our voic - es raise,

All man - kind shall be u - nit - ed,

Let us join in grate - ful praise.

May our hope and strength nev-er fal - ter

Though through the dark our paths may lead.

Sing___ we now in joy and glad-ness

Faith and love shall con - quer greed.

Do You Remember?

Reading music depends on recognizing signs and knowing what they mean.
Find these musical signs in the songs you have learned:

You have been singing and playing in three major keys.
Name these keys and their home tones.

The letter used in naming each home tone is the same letter used in naming each key.

You have learned that a note has three names: $\begin{cases} \text{numeral} \\ \text{syllable} \\ \text{letter} \end{cases}$

In each of these three keys the letter name of each note above is the same but the numeral and syllable names are different.
What are they?

Can You Tell?

These measures are taken from songs you have learned.
Can you name the songs?

Music Brings Us Wonderment

When night comes and the stars twinkle in the sky, we look up and feel the wonder of the earth and heavens. In songs, composers may sometimes try to tell us how they feel about this wonder and beauty. The composer Robert Franz wrote such music when he created a song from a poem describing how music can sing of beauty, of stars, of melody, and of love.

For Music

Emanuel Geibel
Freely Translated

Op. 10, No. 1
Robert Franz

Now the shad-ows dark - en, man-y stars a - light. ___
In   a world of dream - ing mov-ing with-out   rest, ___

What a breath-less won - der fills the air ___ at night.
Float the stars of heav - en lull-ing me ___ to rest.

Mu-sic sings of star-light spar-kling up a - bove! ___

Mel - o - dy   and   star - light

Al -ways sing ___ of ___ love, They sing of love.

40

Morning and Afternoon

Elizabeth Coatsworth

Willard Brooks

The morn-ing runs on nim-ble feet, It's gone be-fore you see
More than a rip-ple in the grass, A flut-ter in the tree.
The af-ter-noon is more in-clined
To drowse a-long the wall;
Some days it seems to close it's eyes
And scarce-ly move at all.

Tap steady quarter-note beats as you sing the song. Listen!
Does the tempo really change or does it just seem to change?

A blue sky, even though far away, is one of the most beautiful things in the world. Try to sing this song so gently that you will think of soft clouds far away in the blue sky.

Today the Sky Is Very Far Away

M. Bardwell

Irving Lowens

Tenderly

To - day the sky is ver - y far a - way,

So blue it is; _____ So blue it is; _____

And, soft as squir-rels' tails, Float _____ o - ver it,

Like lit - tle sails, _____ Soft _ clouds. _____

42

Clouds

Christina G. Rossetti

Edith Krohner

Andante

White sheep, white sheep, On a blue hill,

When the wind stops You all stand still.

ritard. *f*

When the wind blows You walk a - way slow.

a tempo *p*

White sheep, white sheep, Where do you go?____

Where do you go?_____

Special markings help us to be more expressive when we sing or play.
In songs they help us to express the meaning of the words.

◁ (gradually louder symbol)	gradually louder
▷ (gradually softer symbol)	gradually softer
p	soft (Italian: *piano*)
Andante	moderately slow
ritard.	gradually slower
a tempo	return to the speed before the *ritard.*

43

The rainbow arches in the sky,
But in the earth it ends;
And if you ask the reason why,
They'll tell you, "That depends."

It never comes without the rain,
Nor goes without the sun;
And though you try with might and main,
You'll never catch me one.

David McCord

Boats Sail on the Rivers

Christina G. Rossetti

Carlton Beck

Moderato

Boats sail on the riv - ers, And ships sail on the seas;

But clouds that sail a-cross the sky Are pret-ti-er far than these.

There are bridg - es on the riv - ers,

As pret - ty as you please; —

But the bow that bridg - es heav - en,

poco a poco cresc.   *f*

And ov - er-tops the trees, And builds a road from earth to sky,

dim.   *ritard.*

Is pret-ti- er far than these, Is pret-ti- er far than these.

45

Snowflakes

Ruth-Esther Hillila

Allegretto

I can-not reach the stars, Yet they come down to me,

When in each shin-y snow-flake A lit - tle star I see.

Finger Cymbals

They spar-kle bright-ly,

They drift so light-ly,

I turn my face up

D.C. al Fine

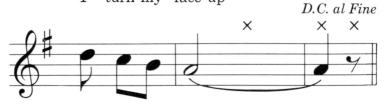

To feel them fall. _____

During his short life, Franz Schubert composed more than 600 songs.
Many of them are among the greatest songs ever written.

Little Snowdrop

F. v. Schober
Translated by Carol B. Pitman

From "*Viola,*" Op. 123
Franz Schubert

Moderato

Lit-tle snow-drop, lit-tle bell, Shar-ing beau-ty where you dwell.

Ris-ing gen-tly by the stream, Nod-ding joy to_ those who dream.

Ring - ing, bring - ing Joy to those who dream.

How many phrases are there in this song?
Which two are most alike?

How are measures five and six similar to measures one and two?
How are they different?

For Listening: "The Snow Is Dancing" from *The Children's Corner Suite* — Debussy
(RCA Victor, ADVENTURES IN MUSIC, Grade 3, Vol. 1)

47

You live in a world of wonder. The sun, the moon, the stars, the earth, oceans and rivers, mountains and canyons — all of these have a special beauty that fills you with wonder. Some children think the moon is the most beautiful of all.

The Quiet Moon

James Stephens

Nathan Saxon

Andante

p

1. The moon comes ev - 'ry night to peep
2. She stands and stares! And then she goes

Through the win - dow where I lie:
To the house that's next to me,

But I pre - tend to be a - sleep;
A - steal - ing by on tip - py toes;

And watch the moon go slow - ly by, —
To peep at folk a - sleep may - be —

pp slower

And she nev - er makes a sound!

For Listening: "Berceuse" from *The Firebird Suite* — Stravinsky
(RCA Victor, ADVENTURES IN MUSIC, Grade 1)

Little Day Moon

Nellie B. Miller

Henry M. Halvorson

Moderato

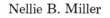

The lit - tle day moon is a toy bal - loon

Lost by a child in its play! ___

It sailed so high It stuck in the sky

And hangs there at half past noon. ___

Which two lines of the song are most alike?
How are they different?

The Little Owlet

George K. Seiler

Allegretto

Lone-ly lit-tle owl - et, In the lin-den tree,

Through the dark your call - ing Seems to sad-den me.

Yet I know I'll miss you, Lone-ly will I be

When no more you're call-ing From the lin - den tree.

Frame the first six notes in each line of the melody.
How are they the same? How are they different?

Ladybug

Translated

German Folk Song
Arr. by Johannes Brahms

Andante

1. O la-dy-bug come here and stand up-on my hand,__
2. O la-dy-bug go fly a-way; your home is burn-ing,

I will not harm you, and noth-ing need a-larm you;
Your chil-dren yearn-ing; they need you, ah, so sad-ly;

I want to see your lit-tle wings;
The wick-ed spi-der spins his net,

The ti-ny, dain-ty col-or'd things,
Your lit-tle chil-dren cry and fret,

poco ritard.

Black and or-ange, red and yel-low, pret-ty fel-low.
For they need you, and will greet you, ah, so glad-ly.

3. O ladybug come back again; the neighbor children
Will never harm you, and nothing need alarm you;
They too would see your little wings;
The tiny, dainty colored things,
Black and orange, red and yellow, pretty fellow.

51

Secret Gardens

Adagio

1. Love - ly se - cret gar - dens grow Un - der-neath the sea, —
2. Mag - ic wreaths of cor - al form Un - der-neath the sea, —

Where the breez - es nev - er blow, Where the stars nev - er show.
'Mid the o - cean cur-rents warm, Safe from wave, safe from storm.

Love - ly se - cret gar - dens grow Un - der-neath the sea. —
Mag - ic wreaths of cor - al form Un - der-neath the sea. —

The mysteries of life under the sea can fill you with a feeling of wonder.
A beautiful melody can do the same thing.

The Magical Sound of Music

What is sound? Sound is anything that can be heard.

Sound is produced by making something *vibrate*, or move back and forth, very rapidly. This movement sets up vibrations in the air, sometimes called sound waves, which move from the thing that causes them to the ear that hears them.

Sound waves may travel in all directions very much as ripples move through still water when a stone is dropped into it. But the ripples are on the surface of the water while the sound waves are in the air.

When sound waves travel through the air and reach your ear, they make your eardrum vibrate. From your eardrum, nerves carry the message to your brain and you hear sound!

Sounds which have a definite pitch have a regular number of vibrations per second. Higher sounds have faster vibrations. Lower sounds have slower vibrations. Most musical instruments produce sounds of definite pitch.

The Symphony Orchestra

The sound of the symphony orchestra is one of the most wonderful sounds that can ever reach your ears. It may come to you through your television, radio, or record player. It may come to you as you sit in a concert hall and hear, as well as see, the many instruments of the orchestra as they make musical sounds for your pleasure.

The symphony orchestras in our country and in many other countries represent man's greatest achievement in producing beautiful sounds.

When you first hear the symphony orchestra it may sound like one great musical sound. Then, as you become better acquainted with the instruments, you will realize that there are four closely related families of instruments within the large orchestra.

Gradually, you will learn to recognize the larger and smaller instruments of the string family that makes up the foundation of the orchestra. You will want to know the brass, woodwind, and percussion families of instruments, for they too make important contributions to the sound of the symphony orchestra.

When so many musicians play together on instruments of many kinds and perform the music of the world's great composers, the sound that comes to your ears is truly the magical sound of music!

THE BOSTON POPS ORCHESTRA

Photograph by Milton Feinberg

The Violin

The violin is the smallest member of the string family.

Its four strings (tuned to G, D, A, and E on the treble staff) are held up by a bridge so they can vibrate when the bow is drawn across them. The player moves the fingers of his left hand above the strings, pressing them down at the right place to change the pitch. Playing on an "open" string will also produce a pitch.

The bow is made of wood with horsehair stretched between its ends. A string is set in vibration by moving the bow across it with the right hand. The composer puts the Italian word *arco* above the music when he wants the player to use the bow. When he wants the strings to be plucked, *pizzicato* is used.

A symphony orchestra may have as many as thirty violins. They are divided into first and second sections. The instruments are the same, but the music they play is usually different. Can you find a violin in the photograph on pages 54 and 55?

Violins are made in smaller sizes for younger children. Perhaps you will have a chance to play one some day.

For Listening: *Instruments of the Orchestra*
(RCA Victor, LE–6000)

Variations on a Theme by Corelli–Tartini
(RCA Victor, LM–2671)

The Cello

Three other members of the string family are the viola, the cello, and the double bass. The cello is one of the larger instruments.

The player is always seated when in a playing position. The instrument rests on the floor between the player's knees.

There are four strings on the cello. They are tuned to C, G, D, and A on the bass clef. The player moves the fingers of his left hand above the strings, pressing them down at the right place to change the pitch.

The bow of the cello is shorter and heavier than the violin bow. A string is set in vibration by moving the bow across it with the right hand. Sometimes a string is made to vibrate by plucking it with the finger.

Cellos are made in half and three-quarter sizes for younger players. Perhaps you will have a chance to play one some day.

There are usually ten cellos in a symphony orchestra. Can you find one in the photograph on pages 54 and 55?

For Listening:

Instruments of the Orchestra
(RCA Victor, LE–6000)

"The Swan" from *The Carnival of the Animals*–Saint-Saëns
(RCA Victor, ADVENTURES IN MUSIC, Grade 3, Vol. 1)

The Flute

The flute is a member of the woodwind family even though it is made of metal.

In early days the flute was made of bamboo or hollow bone. Later, it was made of wood. Today, however, the flute is usually made of silver.

The modern flute is held in a horizontal position to the right side of the player.

Sound is made by blowing air across the hole in the top of the flute near its left end. The air column inside the flute vibrates and produces a tone. Different pitches are made by pressing or releasing keys that close or open holes along the side of the flute.

If you can find middle C on the piano and play all the keys within the three octaves above middle C, you will hear most of the tones that can be played on the flute.

Many orchestras use three flutes. Can you find one in the photograph on pages 54 and 55?

For Listening: *Instruments of the Orchestra*
(RCA Victor, LE–6000)

"Badinerie" from Suite No. 2 in B Minor—Bach
(RCA Victor, ADVENTURES IN MUSIC, Grade 3, Vol. 1)

The Clarinet

Some other members of the wood-wind family are the clarinet, the oboe, the English horn, and the bassoon. The clarinet is made of wood and has many keys.

A single reed made of cane is fastened to the mouthpiece of the clarinet. Part of this reed rests on the firm lower lip of the player. The tip of the reed is set in vibration by the tongue and breath.

The clarinet is held by placing the right thumb under the lower section of the instrument. The left thumb is used to cover the hole or open the register key under the upper section of the instrument. When the register key is open, higher tones may be played. The fingers are held over certain holes or keys. The holes are opened or closed to produce differences in pitch.

There are usually two or three clarinets in a symphony orchestra. Can you find one in the photograph on pages 54 and 55?

For Listening:

Instruments of the Orchestra
(RCA Victor, LE-6000)

Clarinet Concerto in A—Mozart
(RCA Victor, LM-2073)

The Trumpet

Four members of the brass family are the trumpet, the French horn, the trombone, and the tuba. The trumpet is the highest sounding instrument in this family and is made of brass.

In early times the trumpet had no valves. Only "open" tones, as produced on the bugle, could be played on it. Today, the trumpet has three valves, making it possible to play between the open tones.

The instrument is held by the left hand. Three fingers of the right hand are used to press down the valves allowing the air to flow through more tubing. If the trumpet were stretched out in one long piece, it would be about four and one-half feet long.

To produce a tone, the player makes his lips vibrate on the cup-shaped mouthpiece. When the lips are stretched from side to side and are very firm, the tone will be high. When the lips are not as tight, the tone will be lower. Differences in pitch are created by changing the tension of the lips on the mouthpiece and by pressing the valves.

There are usually three trumpets in a symphony orchestra. Can you find one in the photograph on pages 54 and 55?

For Listening: *Instruments of the Orchestra*
(RCA Victor, LE–6000)

Trumpet Concerto in E♭—Haydn
(RCA Victor, LM–2729)

The Snare Drum

The snare drum is one of the smaller drums in the percussion family.

The body of the drum is made of metal or wood. Each open end is covered by animal skin or a thin sheet of plastic, the plastic covering being more common today. The top "head" is called the batter head. Cords of metal or catgut, called snares, are stretched across the bottom head. This head is thinner than the top head.

The snare drum is played by striking the batter head with drumsticks. This makes the air vibrate inside the drum. The vibrating air sets up vibrations in the bottom head and in the snares themselves. When the snares are loosened, the drum sounds like an Indian tom-tom.

How many snare drums do you think are used in the symphony orchestra?

Some other instruments in the percussion family are timpani, bass drum, cymbals, triangle, wood block, and tambourine. Can you find any of them in the photograph on pages 54 and 55?

For Listening:

Instruments of the Orchestra
(RCA Victor, LE–6000)

Marches in Hi-Fi—Boston Pops Orchestra
(RCA Victor, LM–2229)

Your Voice

Each instrument of the symphony orchestra is made by a master craftsman. Some instruments may cost hundreds of dollars.

Did you know that you have an instrument that doesn't cost anything? It's your voice. Everyone has a voice which is used for singing as well as speaking.

Do you know how sound is produced by your voice?

In your throat are two small muscles called vocal cords. They vibrate as the breath passes through them. This sets the air into motion.

Place your fingers on your throat as you hum or sing a tone. Can you feel your vocal cords vibrating?

In speaking or singing you use your breath, tongue, lips, and mouth to shape and control each sound. In this way you can produce musical sounds of different pitches and make them louder or softer.

The sound of your singing voice can be just as beautiful as the sound of the finest instruments in the orchestra. You don't have to use a bow or a reed or a mouthpiece. Your singing "instrument" is always with you. So sing and make your own magical sound of music.

Matching Game

Match the name of each instrument with the correct name of the object which produces the sound of that instrument.

INSTRUMENT	SOUND-PRODUCER
violin	reed
trumpet	vocal cords
drum	strings
cello	lips
flute	batter head
voice	air column
clarinet	strings

Walt Disney's
MARY POPPINS

Based on the books by P. L. Travers

There was trouble in the Banks household at No. 17 Cherry Tree Lane in London. Mrs. Banks was terribly upset and Mr. Banks was furious. It was all because the nursemaid was quitting her job. She was the sixth nanny to leave in four months. Jane and Michael, the children, were very sorry about all the fuss. They wrote a letter to the newspaper to help their father find them a new nanny—just the kind they wanted.

The Perfect Nanny[1]

Richard M. Sherman
Robert B. Sherman

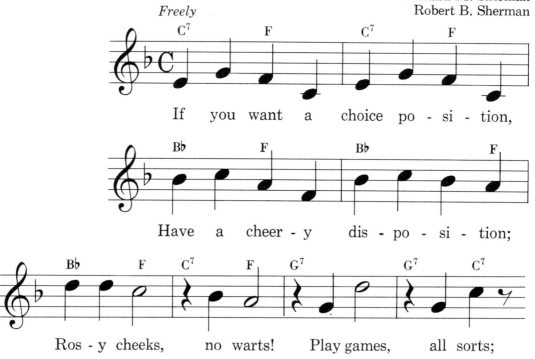

Freely

If you want a choice po - si - tion,

Have a cheer - y dis - po - si - tion;

Ros - y cheeks, no warts! Play games, all sorts;

[1]Condensed from the original song.

If you don't scold and dom - i - nate us,

We will nev - er give you cause to hate us;

We won't hide your spec - ta - cles so you can't see,

Put toads in your bed or pep - per in your tea.

Hur - ry, Nan - ny! Man - y thanks. Sin - cere - ly,

Jane and Mich - ael Banks.

Now that wasn't the kind of nursemaid that Mr. Banks had in mind at all. Angrily he tore up the letter and threw it into the fireplace. But mysteriously and magically the little bits of paper blew up the chimney into the night sky and put themselves together again.

The next morning who should come sailing along on the east wind, with a green umbrella in one hand and the children's letter in the other, but just exactly the person the children had asked for. She landed right at the door of No. 17, marched in, presented herself to Mr. Banks, and engaged herself to be the new nanny.

"My name," she announced, "is Mary Poppins."

Jane and Michael were delighted. They were a little surprised when she slid up the banister to the second floor. They were even more surprised when she unpacked everything, from a mirror to a lamp, out of a carpet bag that appeared to be empty. But when she sang a little song and the whole nursery straightened itself up, they couldn't believe their eyes.

In every job that must be done
There is an element of fun;
You find the fun and snap!
The job's a game;

And every task you undertake
Becomes a piece of cake,
A lark! A spree!
It's very clear to see—

A Spoonful of Sugar

Richard M. Sherman
Robert B. Sherman

Brightly

That a spoon-ful of su-gar helps the med-i-cine go down,

The med-i-cine go down,— med-i-cine go down.

Just a spoon-ful of su-gar helps the med-i-cine go down

In a most de-light-ful way. ____

It was a wonderful, magical thing to see the beds making themselves and the toys putting themselves away.

"Oh, you will stay, won't you, Mary Poppins?" the children begged.

"I'll stay until the wind changes," she told them. "Now on with your coats and hats. We're off for an outing in the park."

There they found Bert, who seemed to be an old friend of Mary Poppins. Bert could do a great many things. Sometimes he was a musician and sometimes a chimney sweep or a kite seller, but this morning he was drawing pictures in colored chalk on the sidewalk. He was delighted to see Mary Poppins. He knew that when she turned up there would be magic and fun, and you might find yourself in places of which you never dreamed.

"Let's have a holiday inside one of my pictures," Bert suggested.

So he took the children's hands and they all jumped. But nothing happened until Mary Poppins said a simple "One, two, three," and there they were, right inside a picture of an English countryside, with a little country fair down the road.

What a glorious day it was! After dancing and tea they got on a merry-go-round, and their wooden horses pranced right off into a fox hunt. Finally they found themselves in the middle of a horse race, and who do you think won? Why, Mary Poppins, of course.

When the newspaper reporters were taking her picture, one of them said, "There probably isn't a word that can describe your happy feelings at winning this race."

But Mary Poppins answered, "There is a perfectly good word."

Supercalifragilisticexpialidocious

Richard M. Sherman
Robert B. Sherman

Brightly

1. Sup - er - cal - i - frag - il - is - tic - ex - pi - al - i - do - cious!
2. Sup - er - cal - i - frag - il - is - tic - ex - pi - al - i - do - cious!

E - ven though the sound of it is some - thing quite a - tro - cious,
Sup - er - cal - i - frag - il - is - tic - ex - pi - al - i - do - cious,

If you say it loud e - nough, you'll al - ways sound pre - co - cious,
Sup - er - cal - i - frag - il - is - tic - ex - pi - al - i - do - cious,

Sup - er - cal - i - frag - il - is - tic - ex - pi - al - i - do - cious!

Even the best days must end, and when it started raining, they found themselves back on the sidewalk in London again. The beautiful drawings were nothing but colorful puddles.

One evening Mary Poppins suggested to Mr. Banks that he take the children on a visit to the bank where he worked. At bedtime she told them that on their way they would pass St. Paul's Cathedral. On the steps they would see the old Bird Woman selling her bags of crumbs for two pennies, or tuppence, to feed the birds. Sure enough, in the morning when they passed the steps, there sat the Bird Woman.

Feed the Birds[1]

Richard M. Sherman
Robert B. Sherman

Feed ___ the birds, tup - pence ___ a bag,

Tup - pence, tup - pence, tup - pence, ___ a bag.

Feed ___ the birds, tup - pence ___ a bag,

Tup - pence, tup - pence, tup - pence a bag.

[1]Condensed from the original song.

Michael wanted to spend the tuppence from his money box to buy some crumbs.

But Mr. Banks said, "No, Michael. When we get to the bank I'll show you what can be done with your tuppence to earn money."

Jane and Michael didn't like the stuffy, dark bank or the bankers at all. When the children made a commotion and ran away, Mr. Banks was in disgrace.

Bert was working as a chimney sweep that day and found Jane and Michael in a London alley. When they explained to him what had happened, Bert said, "Now look at it this way. There's your father, inside that bank day after day. You've got your mother and Mary Poppins and me to look after you. But who looks after your father, tell me that? I think he could do with a bit of help." So Bert took them home and began sweeping their chimney, singing as he worked.

Chim Chim Cher-ee

Richard M. Sherman
Robert B. Sherman

Lightly

Chim chim-in - ey,   chim chim-in - ey,   chim chim   cher - ee!

A   sweep   is   as   luck - y,   as   luck - y   can   be.

Chim chim-in - ey,   chim chim-in - ey,   chim chim   cher - oo!

Good luck will rub off when I shake hands with you,

Or blow me a kiss and that's luck-y, too,

Chim chim-in-ey, chim chim-in-ey, chim chim cher-ee!

When you're with a sweep you're in glad com-pa-ny.

No-where can you find a hap-pi-er crew;

They're all sing-ing, "Chim chim cher-ee, chim cher-oo!"

Chim chim-in-ey, chim chim, cher-ee, chim cher-oo!

Suddenly, just like magic, Michael popped up the chimney with Jane right after him, then Mary Poppins, then Bert. They were all covered with soot and looked just fine.

Bert called out "Cheroo-oo-oo."

From the chimneys all around came answering calls from his pals, the chimney sweeps, "Cheroo-cheroo-cheroo."

Everyone started dancing on the roof.

Step in Time

Richard M. Sherman
Robert B. Sherman

1. Kick your knees up, step in time!
2. Link your el - bows, step in time!

Kick your knees up, step in time!
Link your el - bows, step in time!

Nev - er need a rea - son, nev - er need a rhyme,
Nev - er need a rea - son, nev - er need a rhyme,

Kick your knees up, step in time!
Link your el - bows, step in time!

3. Spin about and step in time! . . .

4. 'Round the chimney step in time! . . .

The dancing didn't stop there. Everybody jumped down Jane and Michael's chimney and danced in the Banks house, with Mrs. Banks joining right in. Everything was gay until the door opened and there stood Mr. Banks, very angry indeed. All the chimney sweeps shook his hand for luck and then left.

"What's going on here?" Mr. Banks shouted. "Mary Poppins, will you be good enough to explain?"

But Mary Poppins replied, "I never explain anything," and she took the children upstairs.

Bert turned to Mr. Banks and said, "You know, sir, what Mary Poppins does say is, 'A spoonful of sugar helps the medicine go down.'"

While Mr. Banks was thinking about that, Michael came downstairs with Jane to say good night to his father. He handed his father his tuppence and hoped that that would make things right. Mr. Banks stood there with a wondering look in his eye.

Later that night he was called down to the bank and was told he had lost his job. He didn't even care. "Supercalifragilisticexpialidocious" was all he said, and he turned and danced his way out of the bank.

Next morning, Mr. Banks came up from the basement with a mended kite in his hand.

"Michael, Jane," he called, "there's a fine west wind blowing. Let's go to the park."

Up in the nursery the children were very upset because Mary Poppins was packing her magic bag to leave. Remember, she had promised to stay only until the wind changed.

"Your father is calling you. Run along, spit-spot," she told them.

So run they did. Mary Poppins watched them go and smiled. The Banks family was a happy one now, and Mr. Banks was singing.

Let's Go Fly a Kite

Richard M. Sherman
Robert B. Sherman

Let's go fly a kite

Up to the high - est height!

Let's go fly a kite

And send it soar - ing

78

Up through the at - mos - phere,

Up where the air is clear.

Oh, let's go go fly a

kite!

It seemed that everybody was flying kites in the park—Bert was there, and Mrs. Banks, and Michael and Jane, and the chimney sweeps, and even the bankers, who gave Mr. Banks his job back again.

And where was Mary Poppins? Why she was flying away with her green umbrella among the kites in the sky over London. But she will come back again some day. Mary Poppins always comes back when she is needed, with her spoonful of sugar, to help children anywhere in the world—maybe even you.

A Spoonful of Sugar

Richard M. Sherman
Robert B. Sherman

For a spoon-ful of su-gar helps the med-i-cine go down,

The med-i-cine go down, med-i-cine go down.

Just a spoon-ful of su-gar helps the med-i-cine go down

In a most de-light-ful way.____

THE END

80

Music Helps Us Celebrate

Fiesta Day

Katherine S. Bolt

Gaily

Dolores Batres G.

On the day of *fi - es - ta,* Wake to see the bright sun,

Hear the ring-ing of church bells; Now *fi - es - ta*'s be - gun.

"*¡Bue-nos dí-as!*" we will say, "What a hap-py hol - i - day!

Come, *a - mi-gos,* let's be gay On *fi - es - ta* day."

The word *fiesta* (pronounced *fee-ehs'-tah*) means "festival," or "celebration."

¡Buenos días! (pronounced *bway'-nohs dee'-ahs*) means "Good day!"

The word *amigos* (pronounced *ah-mee'-gohs*) means "friends."

Fiesta Day

(Instruments)

Bells (1)

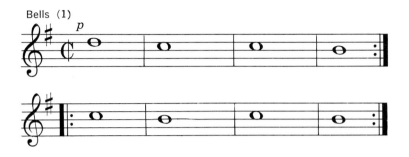

Bells (2)

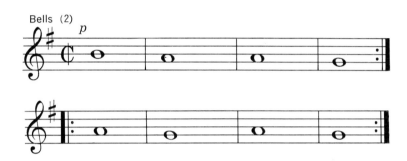

Play the bell parts throughout the song.

Maracas
or
Tambourine

Wood Block
or
Small Drum

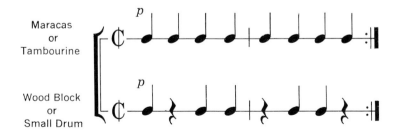

Play the percussion score as an introduction and throughout the song.

83

The Call of the Ocean

Mary E. McIntire

Dreamily

Chris - to - pher Co - lum - bus, The o - cean beck - ons you; —

You shall be a sail - or And make your dreams come true. —

Be strong and brave and faith-ful, Though trou-bles come your way. —

Chris - to - pher Co - lum - bus, The o - cean calls to - day. —

Columbus

R. Ena Butler

Co-lum-bus sailed the o-cean blue in four-teen nine-ty - two, —

And through the years a lot of oth - er peo - ple did it too. —

So here am I and here are you, in this great land of ours; —

Now aren't you glad Co-lum-bus sailed in four-teen nine-ty - two! —

This sign is a *hold* or *fermata*: 𝄐
It tells you to hold the note a little longer than usual.

Halloween

Marguerite Gode

Dennis Krohn

1. A mean old witch with a point-ed hat,
2. A brown-ie elf cried, __ "Peek-a-boo!"

A big straw broom and a fierce black cat,
A round-eyed owl in the tree cried, "Whoo!"

Went __ rid-ing through the __ mid-night sky,
And the chil-dren laughed as they scam-per'd by,

On the night called Hal-low-een,

On the night called Hal-low-een.

You can feel the mood of Halloween in this song.
The tones of the melody were chosen from a *minor scale*.

86

I spot the hills
With yellow balls in autumn.
I light the prairie cornfields
Orange and tawny gold clusters
And I am called pumpkins.

On the last of October
When dusk is fallen
Children join hands
And circle round me
Singing ghost songs
And love to the harvest moon;
I am a jack-o'-lantern
With terrible teeth
And the children know
I am fooling.

Carl Sandburg

The Jack-o'-lantern

Ruth-Esther Hillila

Allegro

1. They picked me out from all the rest,
2. Then when my light was burn - ing bright,

They said I looked the ver - y best.
They took me out in - to the night.

They carved a face with smile so wide,
The wind was howl - ing loud and wild,

And let a can - dle glow in - side.
But I just brave - ly smiled and smiled.

HALLOWEEN

Tonight is the night
When dead leaves fly
Like witches on switches
Across the sky,
When elf and sprite
Flit through the night
On a moony sheen.

Tonight is the night
When leaves make a sound
Like a gnome in his home
Under the ground,
When spooks and trolls
Creep out of holes
Mossy and green.

Tonight is the night
When pumpkins stare
Through sheaves and leaves
Everywhere,
When ghoul and ghost
And goblin host
Dance round their queen.
It's Halloween!

Harry Behn

Composers create beautiful sounds and rhythms with notes.
Poets create beautiful sounds and rhythms with words.

To bring out the sound effects in this poem:

— listen for the variety of sounds and rhythms in the words

— a verse-speaking choir could read the poem

— add appropriate percussion instruments.

88

For Listening: "Hut on Fowl's Legs" from *Pictures at an Exhibition* — Moussorgsky, Ravel.
The composer suggests the flight of Baba Yaga, the fearful witch of Russian folklore.
What kind of sounds and rhythms do you find in the music? How do they compare with
the sounds and rhythms of the poem?

Praise and Thanksgiving

Adapted by
Edith Lovell Thomas

Traditional
Alsatian Round

Allegretto

Praise and thanks - giv - ing let ev - 'ry - one bring

Un - to our Fa - ther for ev - 'ry good thing.

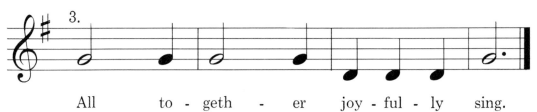

All to - geth - er joy - ful - ly sing.

Singing rounds can be a fine musical adventure for you.
Make sure that you know the song before singing it as a round.

Play the following chord pattern for autoharp throughout the song.
It will help you to sing in tune and to keep together.

$\frac{3}{4}$ G — — | G — — | D⁷ — — | G — — :‖

Our Thanks

E. B. Kay

1. For the world so fair, For Thy lov - ing care,

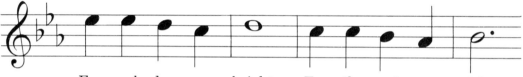

For each day so bright, For the qui - et night,

Our thanks to Thee we sing, Our thanks for ev - 'ry - thing.

2. For a spring song heard
   From a singing bird,
   For the shining hours,
   Sweet with fragrant flow'rs,
   Our thanks to Thee we sing,
   Our thanks for ev'rything.

3. For a lovely star,
   Twinkling from afar,
   For the moonbeams bright,
   Shimm'ring through the night,
   Our thanks to Thee we sing,
   Our thanks for ev'rything.

A composer often uses Italian words to tell you how to sing or play his music.

Adagio	slow
legato	smooth and flowing
ritard.	become slower

Thanksgiving Day

Lydia Maria Child   Unknown

Gaily

O - ver the riv - er and through the wood,

To grand-fa-ther's house we go. _____

The horse knows the way to car - ry the sleigh

Through the white and drift - ed snow. ___

Wood Block

Jingle Clogs

Play as an introduction and throughout the song.

O - ver the riv - er and through the wood,

Oh, how the wind does blow! _____

It stings the toes and bites the nose,

As o - ver the ground we go. _____

I'm glad that it's Thanksgiving Day
And all the world is merry,
And I am glad I have a fork
And that the pie is cherry.

Marchette Chute

On each of the eight days of Hanukkah a candle in the menorah is lighted to celebrate a miracle which happened long ago.

Light a Little Candle

Rose Engel
Judith Berman

Folk Melody
Adapted

Allegretto

Light a lit - tle can - dle, Ha - nuk - kah will come;

Eat a lit - tle lat - ke, Yum, yum, yum, yum, yum!

I'm count-ing on my fin-gers and I'm count-ing on my thumb,

Just how man - y days till Ha - nuk - kah will come!

Hanukkah (pronounced *Hah'-noo-kuh*) is an eight-day Jewish holiday.

A latke (pronounced *laht'-keh*) is a pancake.

A menorah (pronounced *meh-noh'-ruh*) is an eight-branched candelabrum.

Notice the two different tempo markings in this song.

Make up a tambourine part for the refrain.

It's Hanukkah!

C. N. Bialik
Adapted

"Lichvod Hachanukah"
Shalom Altman

1. The can - dles shine on ___ high,

The can - dles shine on ___ high.

Do you know the rea - son ___ why?

REFRAIN
Allegro

Be - cause, be - cause, be - cause it's Ha - nuk - kah, ___

Be - cause, be - cause, be - cause it's Ha - nuk - kah!

2. A dreydl I will buy, . . .   3. Let's have a pancake fry, . . .

A dreydl (pronounced *dray'-dl*) is a top.

Hear the carols . . .   See the candles . . .   Feel its blessing . . .
Hear the bells . . .   Watch a star   Sense its power . . .
Know the story   Twinkle "Christmas"   Christmas . . . Christmas!
Christmas tells!   From afar.   Timeless hour!

Lois Snelling

Long Ago

L. E. W.   French Folk Melody

Moderato

1. Long, long a - go there came a star
2. Long, long a - go the an - gels sang,

O - ver   Beth-le - hem a - far,
From   on   high their voic-es rang.

Guid-ing men of old   With their gifts of gold
On that ho - ly day   Shep-herds came to pray,

To the low - ly sta-ble Through the dark and cold.
Kneel-ing by the man - ger Where the Ba - by lay.

Oxen, Oxen

Freely Translated and
Adapted by H. F. G.

Italian Melody

Andante

1, 2. "Ox - en, ox - en, walk - ing so slow - ly,

Where do you go on this dark night?"

1. "An - gels sing to shep-herds so low - ly,
2. "In a man - ger sleeps the Child Ho - ly,

'Fol - low the star that shines so bright.'"
For this a star shall give its light."

Lul - la - by, Lul - la - by.

We Three Kings of Orient Are

John H. Hopkins, Jr.

Andante

We three kings of O - ri - ent are;

Bear - ing gifts we tra - verse a - far

Field and foun - tain, moor and moun - tain,

REFRAIN

Fol-low-ing yon - der star. O____

Star of won-der, star of night, Star with roy - al beau-ty bright,

West-ward lead-ing, still pro-ceed-ing, Guide us to thy per-fect light.

How Far Is It to Bethlehem?

Frances Chesterton

English Folk Melody

Andante

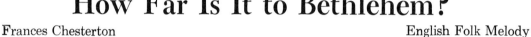

1. How far is it to Beth - le-hem? Not ver - y far.
2. May we stroke the crea-tures there, Ox, ass, or sheep?

Shall we find the sta - ble-room Lit by a star?
May we peep like them and see Je - sus a - sleep?

Can we see the lit - tle Child, Is He with - in?
If we touch His ti - ny hand Will He a - wake?

If __ we lift the wood-en latch May we go in?
Will __ He know we've come so far Just for His sake?

A little child
   A shining star
A stable rude
   A door ajar.

Yet in that place
   So crude, forlorn,
The hope of all
   The world was born.

Unknown

The Friendly Beasts

Twelfth-Century Carol

Andante

1. Je - sus our broth - er, kind and good,

Was hum - bly born in a sta - ble rude;

The friend - ly beasts a - round Him stood,

Je - sus our broth - er, kind and good.

2. "I," said the donkey, shaggy and brown,
   "I carried His mother up hill and down;
   I carried His mother to Bethlehem town.
   I," said the donkey, shaggy and brown.

3. "I," said the cow all white and red,
   "I gave Him my manger for His bed,
   I gave Him my hay to pillow His head.
   I," said the cow all white and red.

4. "I," said the sheep with curly horn,
   "I gave Him my wool for His blanket warm.
   He wore my coat on Christmas morn.
   I," said the sheep with curly horn.

5. "I," said the dove from the rafters high,
   "I cooed Him to sleep that He should not cry,
   We cooed Him to sleep, my mate and I.
   I," said the dove from the rafters high.

6. Thus every beast, by some good spell,
   In the stable dark was glad to tell
   Of the gift that he gave Emmanuel.
   The gift that he gave Emmanuel.

Carol of the Sheep Dog

Norma B. Sorlien

Andante

1. I went to see the Christ Child on that first Christ-mas day.
2. Kind Jo-seph gave me wa - ter and Ma - ry strok'd my head.

The shep-herds walked be-fore me, a star to guide their way.
The Ba - by Je - sus slum-ber'd, with me to guard his bed.

I crept up to the man - ger, I lay down in the hay,
If He be-comes a shep - herd and gath - ers lambs to fold,

For I'm a shep-herd's sheep dog that fetch - es sheep that stray.
Per - haps He'll need a sheep dog, I hope I'm not too old!

Gentle is He | As a stream of water | Such is He
As windless snow. | In August heat, | Who is born this day
Kind as a tree | As a blueberry bush | In Bethlehem
With shelter below, | Hidden and sweet, | So far away!

Elizabeth Coatsworth

O Jesu Sweet

English Version by
Christine Turner Curtis

Old German Hymn Melody

1. O Je - su[1] sweet, O Je - su mild,
2. O Je - su sweet, O Je - su mild,

Thou art the Fa - ther's ho - ly Child,
Thy Moth - er looked on Thee and smiled,

From heav'n come down to do His will,
Then sent Thee forth with man to share,

His lov - ing pur - pose to ful - fill.
This life of sor - row and of care.

O Je - su sweet, O Je - su mild.
O Je - su sweet, O Je - su mild.

[1] Pronounced *yay'-zoo.*

103

Rocking

Translated

Czech Carol

Moderato

1. Lit - tle Je - sus, sweet-ly___ sleep, do not___ stir;
2. Ma - ry's lit - tle ba - by___ sleep, sweet - ly ___ sleep,

We will ___ lend a ___ coat of ___ fur,
Sleep in ___ com - fort, ___ slum - ber ___ deep;

We will rock you, rock you, rock you,

We will rock you, rock you, rock you:

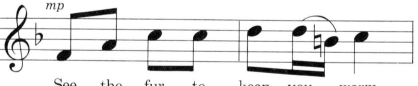

See the fur to keep you ___ warm,
We will serve you all we ___ can,

Snug - ly ___ round your ___ ti - ny ___ form.
Dar - ling, ___ dar - ling, ___ lit - tle ___ man.

A New Year's Greeting

Adapted by
Katherine S. Bolt

"Kado Matsu"
Old Japanese Song

Happily

"O - me - de - to go - zai mas,[1]" we will bow and say,

"O - me - de - to go - zai mas," hap - py New Year's Day.

Let us place our pine branch - es here be - side the door,

And wish our friends and neigh - bors man - y new years more.

[1]Pronounced *oh-meh-deh-toh goh-zy mahs.*

New Year's Day in Japan is a very happy holiday. Many people welcome the rising sun by clapping their hands and bowing to it. The children usually wear new clothes. They go walking with their families in the public parks, call on friends and relatives, and exchange gifts. Each home is decorated with pine and bamboo (*kado matsu*). These decorations represent strength and love of country.

Guess Who!

Ena B. Knippel

Here's a heart of red and blue, Guess who sent it just for you.

Guess who! Guess who! O - pen it and you will see,

It's a val - en - tine from me, It's from me! ____

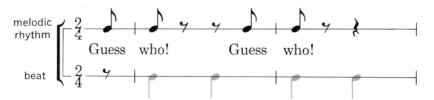

The rests in this song create a feeling of surprise and excitement.
Tap the beat and speak the words of this rhythm pattern.

If apples were pears,
And peaches were plums,
And the rose had a different name,

If tigers were bears,
And fingers were thumbs,
I'd love you just the same!

Unknown

A Valentine Box

R. Ena Butler

A valentine box just full of surprises,
All kinds of valentines, all shapes and sizes.
Some are big and some are small,
But love is written on them all,
Some are for you, and some are for me,
Oh, what a happiness box that will be!

EASTER JOY

Look, everyone, look!
Leaves are lovely on bush and bough,
Robins build in the treetops now,
    A song sounds in the brook!

Run, every child, run!
Flowers are shining by hollow and hill,
Buttercup, violet, daffodil,
    All bright in the sun!

Bells silverly ring!
With grass and flowers and buds uncurled,
Easter is back in the beautiful world —
    Sing, everyone, sing!

Nancy Byrd Turner

Do you feel this way about Easter and springtime?
You might like to make up your own poem.

— First, make a list of your favorite springtime things.
   Use beautiful and rhythmic words that seem to want to sing.

— Weave the words into lines so that you have a poem instead of a story.
   Some poems rhyme; others do not. You may do as you like.

— Read your poem aloud and listen!
   You may hear a melody singing in your mind.

This is how many songs are made.

108

The great composer Ludwig van Beethoven created his melodies in another way. Many stories have been written about Beethoven's love of the beautiful world he lived in and how he enjoyed walking through the countryside. Sometimes, while taking these walks, melodies would sing in his mind and he would write them down in a notebook. Later, he would weave these melodies, or *themes*, into great pieces of music called *symphonies*.

The theme below is from the first movement of Beethoven's Symphony No. 6 ("Pastoral"). It expresses the joy of a walk through the countryside. Some day you will enjoy listening to the whole symphony.

In the Easter Parade

Helen Taylor

Eric Winneger

Moderato

{ Walk-ing in the sun - shine,   stroll-ing in the shade, }
{ Talk-ing with our friends   where   yes - ter - day we played, }

Walk-ing with my fam -'ly   in   the Eas - ter   Pa - rade.

What a hap - py day,   Be - fore the sun can fade,

Walk-ing with my fam -'ly   in   the Eas - ter   Pa - rade.

110

More Music We Can Sing and Play

Music in 6/8 Meter

There are many kinds of music in 6/8 meter. Some music is slow and gentle as a lullaby. Some music seems to hop or gallop and make you think of a rabbit hopping or a pony galloping by. Other music may make you think of a band playing as it goes marching along (left, right; left, right).

Music in 6/8 meter generally has two beats in each measure. The many different kinds of rhythm patterns make the music interesting to see and follow as you sing or play it.

Row, Row, Row Your Boat

E. O. Lyte

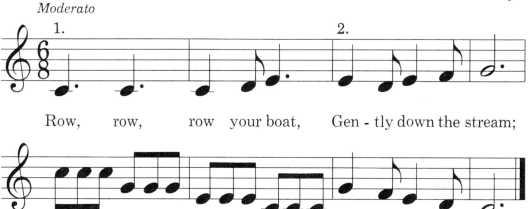

Row, row, row your boat, Gen - tly down the stream;

Mer-ri-ly, mer-ri-ly, mer-ri-ly, mer-ri-ly, Life is but a dream.

Find the measures which have these rhythm patterns.
What are the words?

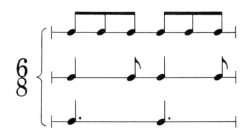

Out on the Ocean

Paraphrased by C. J. C.

From *The Chimes of Normandy*
Robert Planquette

With rock-ing mo - tion, out on the o - cean

Go, gal-lant sail - or - boy, o - cean's your home!

Calm you'll be sleep - ing while gales are sweep - ing.

O'er the great o - cean of wa - ters you roam.

Some of the measures in this song have the same rhythm patterns as in "Row, Row, Row Your Boat." Can you find them?

For Listening: "Barcarolle" from *The Tales of Hoffman*—Offenbach
(RCA Victor, ADVENTURES IN MUSIC, Grade 3, Vol. 1)

How many Mother Goose songs do you remember?
Many of them are written in ⁶₈ meter.
Here are the first two measures from five of them.
Sing each song and clap the melodic rhythm.

1. Lit - tle Jack Horn - er sat in a cor - ner

2. Rock - a - bye, ba - by, on the tree - top.

3. Three blind mice,

4. Hey, did - dle, did - dle! The cat and the fid - dle, The

5. See, saw, Mar - ger - y Daw,

Clap these rhythm patterns.
Can you tell to which song each pattern belongs?

Rig-a-jig-jig

Singing Game

Rig - a - jig-jig, and a -way   we go,   A -

way   we go,   a -way   we go;

Rig - a - jig-jig, and a - way we go, Heigh-o, heigh-o,— heigh-o. ——

Some may clap the rhythm of the melody while others tap the beat.

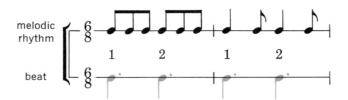

melodic rhythm

1   2   1   2

beat

116

We're All Together Again

Scout Song

In marching tempo

We're all to-geth-er a - gain, We're here, we're here! —

We're all to-geth-er a - gain, We're here, we're here!

Who knows when we'll be all to-geth-er a - gain,

Sing-ing all to-geth-er a - gain, We're here, we're here! —

Select appropriate percussion instruments to play these rhythms.

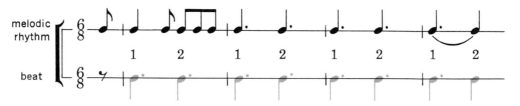

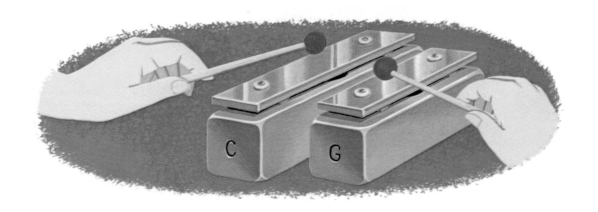

Gold and Silver Bells

Dennis Krohn

The bells that are made of gold and sil - ver

Proud-ly are ring-ing, ding, dong!

Proud-ly are ring-ing, ding, dong! Ding, dong! The dong! Ding, dong!

New Major Keys

This song is in the key of B♭ major.
The home tone (1, or *do*) is B♭.
There are two flats in the key of B♭ major.

Sing, Sing Along

Freely Translated

Moravian Folk Song

Lively

do ti la so fa mi re do

Sing, sing a-long, if you're feel-ing sad.

so

Sing, sing a-long, it will make you glad.

re

If your heart is kind and true, hap-py in the things you do,

do

Then you can sing, sing the whole day through.

Now the key is D major and the home tone is D.
The melody is the same but it looks higher on the staff.
It also sounds higher.

Sing, Sing Along

Freely Translated

Moravian Folk Song

Sing,   sing a - long,   if you're feel - ing   sad.

Sing,   sing a - long,   it will   make   you   glad.

If your heart is kind and true,   hap-py in the things you do,

Then   you can   sing,   sing the   whole   day   through.

Making Up Songs

The stars are shining clear and bright
Like tiny candles in the night.

Jane Tinsley

Read the words and try to feel the beat.
Copy the words beneath the staff on the chalkboard.
Sing the melody as far as it goes.

You may change the rhythm by adding a dot to a quarter note and changing the next quarter note to an eighth note. Read the words in the different rhythm patterns below. Change the rhythm of the music on the chalkboard. Sing the melody with each change made by adding the dot and decide which new rhythm you like best.

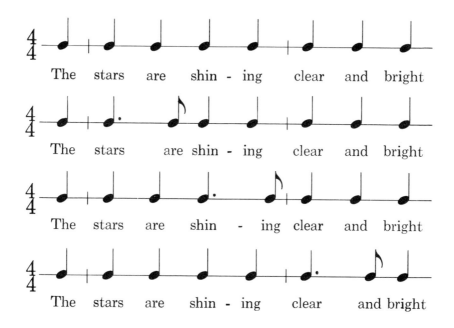

Try to complete the song.

Here is the beginning of the same rhyme.
Now the melody is in 3/4 meter and in a higher key.
Try to complete this melody.
Think of still another way to complete it.

The Stars

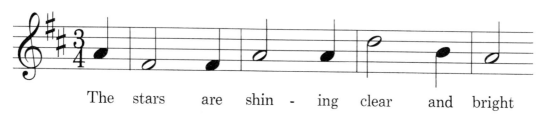

123

Here is another rhyme that you can make into a song.

I have a little boat   A very pleasant task
I sail upon the sea;   Is sailing it for me.

Sarah Jane S. Harrington

My Little Boat

I have a lit - tle boat ___

I sail up - on the sea; ___

A ver - y pleas - ant task ___

Is sail - ing it for me. ___

Try to feel the beat as you read the words. Write them beneath the staff on the chalkboard. Sing the melody with the words as far as it goes; then listen for tones that you might hear for the second line. Write the notes for them on the chalkboard. The third line of melody may sometimes be the same, or nearly the same, as the first line. Sing the melody with the words again as far as it goes; then complete the song in the same way.

Here are three more ways that a melody for the little boat rhyme may begin. How would you like to start your song with one of these ideas? Which one do you like the best?

1.

I have a lit - tle boat____

2.

I __ have a lit - tle boat __

3.

I have a lit - tle boat

You might like to finish all three songs using the beginning given for each. You will be learning to create and write music in different keys and meters. Sing the completed songs. Compare them and choose the one you like the best.

125

Now you may be ready to write complete melodies. When you have selected the poem, read it over and over. The words will help you in discovering which meter to use. Choose the meter you think is best. Some of you may have a good idea for the beginning of the melody. Others may be able to sing the next part of the melody. Sometimes it helps to use the bells or piano when you are making up songs.

FUZZY WUZZY, CREEPY CRAWLY

Fuzzy wuzzy, creepy crawly
Caterpillar funny,
You will be a butterfly
When the days are sunny.

Lillian Schulz

DOWN IN THE HOLLOW

Down in the hollow,
Not so far away,
I saw a little ladybug
When I went to play.

Aileen Fisher

OUTSIDE THE DOOR

Outside the door the bare tree stands,
And catches snowflakes in its hands,
And holds them well and holds them high,
Until a puffing wind comes by.

Annette Wynne

Some Famous Melodies

Here are some melodies to play on the bells or on the piano.

Tallis' Canon

Thomas Tallis

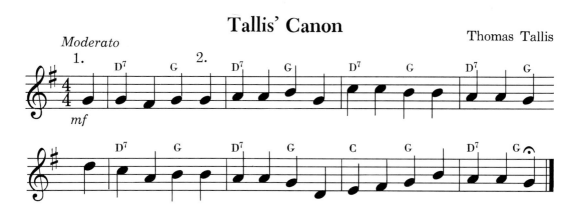

Slumber Song

"Wiegenlied"
Franz Schubert

Minuet in G

Excerpt
Johann Sebastian Bach

Minuet

From *Don Giovanni*
Wolfgang Amadeus Mozart

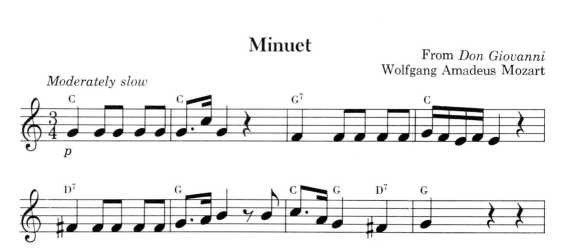

Cradle Song

"Wiegenlied," Op. 49, No. 4
Johannes Brahms

With gentle motion

Grand Waltz

From Op. 18
Frédéric Chopin

Polka[1]

From *Schwanda, the Bagpiper*
Jaromír Weinberger

[1]© Copyright 1929, Universal Edition.
Used by permission of Associated Music Publishers, Inc. and the
Canadian copyright owners, Boosey & Hawkes (Canada) Ltd.

Music of Home and Country

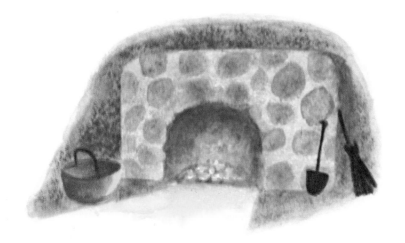

In the Fireplace

Freely Translated
by Frederick Beckman

Jewish Folk Song

Slowly

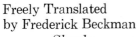

There's a lit-tle glow   in the fire - place Tell-ing   you and   me,

"Time to   go   to bed, you lit-tle sleep-y-head, Close your eyes and dream,

Time to   go   to bed, you lit-tle sleep-y-head, Close your eyes and dream."

Quiet is the night, soft is the breeze,
Dim is the moon over the trees.
Sleep, children, sleep, be not alarmed,
Angels on guard shall keep you unharmed.

Old Rhyme

Sleep

Sarah Jane S. Harrington

Dorothy Stevens

Andante

1. Sleep, my lit - tle one, sleep,_____
2. Sleep, my lit - tle one, sleep,_____

For twin - kling stars___ will light___ the way,
The sil - ver moon___ is watch - ing thee,

To dream - land just___ a dream_ a - way,
Her lit - tle beams___ have come___ to see

So,_ sleep, my lit - tle one, sleep._ Sleep, sleep, sleep.
My_ ba - by go - ing to sleep._ Sleep, sleep, sleep.

Things I Like Best

Ethel Crowninshield

Wolfgang Amadeus Mozart

Not too fast

1. These are the things that I like best:
2. These are the things I'll not for - get,

One bright star and the moon close by;
Things I see when I close my eyes:

I like the sun - set in the west,
My moth - er's face, and friends I've met,

Paint - ing bright col - ors a - cross the sky.
Sun on my wall when it's time to rise.

Sleep, My Little One

English Version by L. E. W.

Jewish Folk Song

Andante

Sleep, my lit - tle one, Sleep, my pret-ty one, Ey_ lu_ lu lu lu.[1]

Sleep, my gen-tle one, Sleep, my dear-est one, Ey_ lu_ lu lu lu.

Dream, my lit - tle one, Dream, my pret-ty one, Ey_ lu_ lu lu lu.

Soon the morn-ing light fol-lows dark-est night, So I sing to you,

Ey__ lu lu lu.

Where does the melody move chordwise?
Where does it move scalewise?

[1]Pronounced *eye loo loo loo loo.*

135

Did you know that cowboys sing lullabies to the cattle out on the range? The little motherless calves, or dogies, rest quietly when they hear this soothing song at night.

Night Herding Song

Cowboy Song

1. Oh, say, lit - tle do - gies, quit rov - ing a - round,
2. Oh, lay down, my do - gies, quit sift - ing a - round,

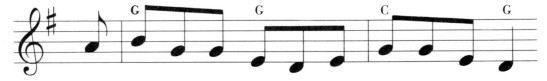

You've wan - dered and tram - pled all o - ver the ground.
Just stretch a - way out on the big o - pen ground.

Oh, graze a - long, do - gies, and move kind - a slow,
My horse is leg - wea - ry and I'm aw - ful tired,

And don't be for - ev - er so much on the go,
If you get a - way, then I'll sure - ly be fired.

Move slow, lit - tle do - gies, move slow. _____
Oh, lay down, my do - gies, lay down. _____

Hi - o, hi - o, __ hi - o. _____
Hi - o, hi - o, __ hi - o. _____

The Butterfly

Translated by
Carol B. Pitman

Op. 79, No. 2
Robert Schumann

Allegro

Bells or Piano

1. Oh, but - ter - fly, say,

Why you fly a - way?

How do you   Fly quick - ly

So near and then far,___ So near and then far?

2. Why don't you stay here,
   So you will be near?
   I'll try not
   To hurt you
   And do you some harm,
   And do you some harm.

3. I have things to say,
   Come closer this way.
   I bring you
   My friendship
   So kind and so true,
   So kind and so true.

138

Susie, Little Susie

Translated

From *Hansel and Gretel*
Engelbert Humperdinck

Allegretto

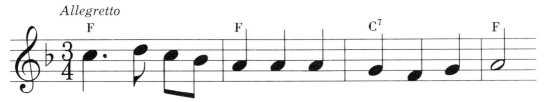

1. Su - sie, lit - tle Su - sie, now   what   is   the   news?
2. Su - sie, lit - tle Su - sie, we   are   in   a   fix,

The   geese   are go - ing bare-foot be - cause they've no shoes.
No   pen - nies for some sug - ar   and   no   bread to   mix.

The   cob - bler   has   leath - er,   but   no   last   to   use,
If   I   sell   my   bed, sleep on   straw   for   the   night,

So   he can-not make them a   pair   of   new   shoes.
Feath - ers will not prick - le   and   fleas   will   not   bite.

Baby Chicks

(*Los Pollitos*)

Freely Translated by K. S. B.

Spanish Folk Song

Allegro

1. Lit - tle ba - by chicks say: "Pí - o, pí - o, pí - o."
   Los po - lli - tos di - cen: "Pí - o, pí - o, pí - o."

When they're feel-ing hun - gry, when they're feel-ing cold. ___
Cuan - do tie - nen ham - bre, cuan - do tie - nen frí - o.

2. "Here's your wheat and barley, *pío, pío, pío,*
   You may eat your supper, all that you can hold."

3. "Sleep until the morning, *pío, pío, pío,*
   Mother knows what's best for chickies one day old."

Pronunciation:

Lohs poh-lyee'-tohs dee'-sehn: "Pee'-oh, pee'-oh, pee'-oh."
Kwahn'-doh tyeh'-nehn ahm'-breh, Kwahn'-doh tyeh'-nehn free'-oh.

Oh, Poor Chick-a-biddy

Freely Translated

German Folk Song
Arr. by Johannes Brahms

Oh,   poor chick-a-bid-dy, chick-a-bid-dy's gone,   where has she gone?

Where is my chick-a-bid-dy, where has she gone?

Have   you seen   my chick-a-bid-dy run-ning?

She   is small,   but she is quick and cun-ning.

Which lines of the melody are exactly the same?
Find where the melody moves chordwise.
Find where the melody moves scalewise.

These notes are *sixteenth notes*:

141

For Health and Strength

Old English Round

For health and strength and dai-ly food, We praise Thy name, O Lord.

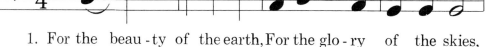

For the Beauty of the Earth

Folliott S. Pierpont

Conrad Kocher
Adapted

1. For the beau-ty of the earth, For the glo-ry of the skies,

For the love which from our birth O-ver and a-round us lies;

Lord of all, to Thee we raise This, our hymn of grate-ful praise.

2. For the wonder of each hour,
   Of the day and of the night,
   Hill and vale, and tree and flower,
   Sun and moon, and stars of light; . . .

3. For the joy of human love,
   Brother, sister, parent, child,
   Friends on earth, and friends above,
   For all gentle thoughts and mild; . . .

142

Aloha Oe

English Version by F. B.

Queen Liliuokalani

REFRAIN

Slowly

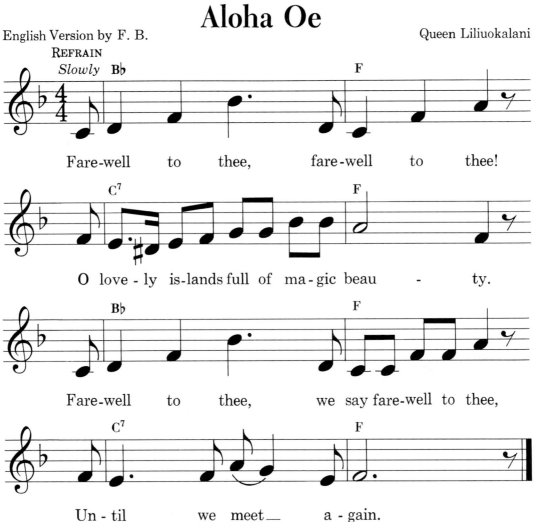

Fare-well to thee, fare-well to thee!

O love-ly is-lands full of ma-gic beau - ty.

Fare-well to thee, we say fare-well to thee,

Un - til we meet a - gain.

America, the Beautiful

Katharine Lee Bates

Samuel A. Ward

Majestically

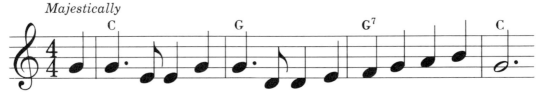

O beau - ti - ful for spa - cious skies, For am - ber waves of grain,

For pur - ple moun - tain maj - es - ties A - bove the fruit - ed plain!

A - mer - i - ca! A - mer - i - ca! God shed His grace on thee,

And crown thy good with broth - er - hood From sea to shin - ing sea!

America

Samuel Francis Smith Traditional

Proudly

My coun-try, 'tis of thee,

Sweet land of lib-er-ty,

Of thee I sing.

Land where my fa-thers died!

Land of the Pil-grims' pride!

From ev-'ry_ moun-tain-side, Let_ free-dom ring!

145

The Star-Spangled Banner

Francis Scott Key   John Stafford Smith

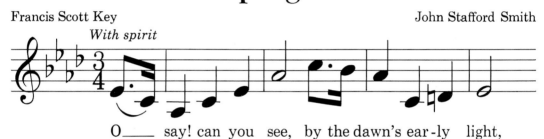

O__ say! can you see, by the dawn's ear-ly light,

What so proud - ly we hail'd at the twi-light's last gleam-ing?

Whose broad stripes and bright stars, thro' the per - il - ous fight,

O'er the ram-parts we watch'd, were so gal-lant - ly stream-ing?

146

And the rock-ets' red glare, the bombs burst-ing in air,

Gave proof thro' the night that our flag was still there.

O say, does that Star-Span-gled Ban-ner _ yet _ wave _

O'er the land __ of the free and the home of the brave?

There Are Many Flags in Many Lands

M. H. Howliston

Unknown

There are man-y flags in man-y lands, There are flags of ev-'ry hue;

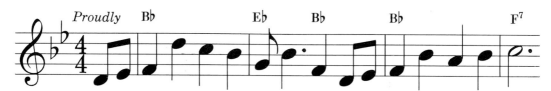

But there is no flag, how-ev-er grand, Like our own Red, White, and Blue.

Then hur-rah for the flag, our coun-try's flag, Its stripes and white stars, too;

There is no flag in an-y land Like our own Red, White, and Blue.

148

Music Makes Us Move

If You're Happy

Action Song

1. If you're hap-py and you know it, clap your hands,

If you're hap-py and you know it, clap your hands,

If you're hap-py and you know it, then your face will sure-ly show it

If you're hap-py and you know it, clap your hands.

2. . . . tap your toe, (*tap, tap*)
3. . . . nod your head, (*down, up*)
4. . . . do all three, (*together*)

150

Tambur Andandori

English Version by
Katherine S. Bolt

Hungarian Folk-Dance Song

Allegro

1. { Dance to gyp-sy   mu-sic play-ing, Tam-bur An-dan - do - ri.[1]
   { Hear the gyp-sy   mu-sic say-ing, Tam-bur An-dan - do - ri.

REFRAIN

Tam-bur-am-bur   An-dan-do - ri,

Tam-bur-am-bur   An-dan-do - ri,

a tempo

Tam-bur An-dan - do - ri.

2. Dance around the leaping fire,
   Tambur Andandori.
   Kick your heels and toes up higher,
   Tambur Andandori. . . .

3. Circle faster and yet faster,
   Tambur Andandori.
   Dance your shoes clear off, young Master,
   Tambur Andandori. . . .

[1]Pronounced *tam'-boor an-dan-doh'-ree.*

151

Three Pirates

English Ballad

Allegro

1. Three pi-rates came to Lon-don Town, Yo ho,— yo ho,—
2. At first they came to Way-side Inn, Yo ho,— yo ho,—

Three pi-rates came to Lon-don Town, Yo ho,— yo ho,—
At first they came to Way-side Inn, Yo ho,— yo ho,—

Three pi-rates came to Lon-don Town,
At first they came to Way-side Inn,

To see the king put on his crown,
And said, "Good land - lord, let us in."

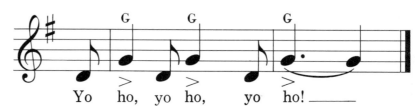

Yo ho, you lub-bers, yo ho, you lub-bers,

Yo ho, yo ho, yo ho!—

3. Oh landlord, have you hoards of gold, . . .
   Enough to fill the after hold? . . .

4. Oh yes, sir, I have hoards of gold, . . .
   Enough to fill the after hold. . . .

5. Oh landlord, have you a daughter fair, . . .
   With laughing eyes and curly hair? . . .

6. Oh yes, sir, I've a daughter fair, . . .
   With laughing eyes and curly hair. . . .

7. Oh landlord, will she marry me, . . .
   And sail with me across the sea? . . .

8. Oh yes, sir, she will marry thee, . . .
   And sail with thee across the sea. . . .

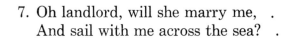

Choose one person to be the "landlord."
Which verses should the "landlord" sing alone?
On "Yo ho, you lubbers, . . . " everyone join in.

153

Apples and Cheese

Freely Translated by
Katherine S. Bolt

Old French Singing Game

Allegretto

Down in the mar-ket of *les Halles*[1]   I   am sell-ing   ap - ples.

Down in the mar-ket of *les Halles*   I   am sell-ing cheese.

Come   buy my   ap - ples,   bright   shin-y   ap - ples.

Come   buy my   ap - ples and buy   my   cheese.

[1]Pronounced *lay ahl.*

Form couples and face one another.
In measure:

1   slap your knees; then clap your hands.
2   clap right hands with your partner; then clap your own hands.
3   slap your knees; then clap your hands.
4   clap left hands with your partner; then clap your own hands.
5-8   repeat movements for measures one through four.
9-12   link right arms with left hand raised; then skip in a circle.
13-16   repeat with left arms linked and right hand up.

How Many Miles to London Town?

Allegro   Old Singing Game

1. "How man - y miles   to   Lon - don town?"
2. "O - pen the gate   and   let   me pass!"

"Four   -   score   and   ten!"_____
"Toll   first   you   pay!"_____

"Can   I   get   there   by   can - dle-light?"
"I   have   no   gold,   what   shall   I   do?"

"Yes!   and   back   a - gain."_____
"Turn   and   go   a - way."_____

Form two lines and face each other.
Leave a wide open space.
One player stands in the middle.
At the end of the song, the children run to the opposite side.
The one in the middle tries to tag as many as possible.
Those who are caught join the player in the middle.
Repeat the game until all are tagged.
The last one to be caught wins the game.

Little Johnny England

Australian Folk Song

Moderato

1,2. Lit - tle John-ny Eng - land, he went a -wan-der-ing;

He went a -wan-der-ing all day long;

He went a -wan-der-ing with his lit - tle pan - ni - kin,[1]

He went a -wan -der-ing all day long.

[1] a tin pan or cup

156

1. You}
2. We} are the butch - ers,

You}
We} are the bak - ers,

You}
We} are the can - dle-stick mak - ers,

You're}
We're} the lin - en weav - ers,

You're}
We're} the lin - en drap - ers,

ALL

You}
We} are the bro - kers, We're all the bro-kers' men.

In the second stanza each group sings its own part, then all join in.

Sandy Girl

Game Song from Trinidad

Andante

There was a lit-tle Sand-y girl Sit-ting on a stone,

Weep - ing, cry - ing, All the day a - lone.

Rise up, Sand - y girl, Wipe your tears a - way,

Choose the one you like the best, And run, run a - way.

Form a circle and join hands.
"Sandy girl (or boy)" sits in the center of the circle.
She makes believe she is weeping as all walk around her.
At "rise up," she wipes the tears away.
Holding her choice by the hand, they run away.
Her choice becomes "Sandy girl (or boy)" the next time.

The Shepherdess

English Version by
Katherine S. Bolt

Old French Song

Lit-tle shep-herd-ess, to-day[1] Count your sheep be-fore they stray.

They are stand-ing in the fold; Just how man-y does it hold?

You must hur-ry, you must hur-ry, Soon the gate will o-pen wide,

And they all will run a-way Out in-to the fields to play.

[1]For a boy, sing "Little shepherd boy, today."

Form a large circle around a blindfolded "shepherdess."
Before the song begins, several children join her in the "sheepfold."
The "shepherdess" tries to discover how many there are.
If she counts right, she may be the "shepherdess" again.

Carousel

Alice Ricky

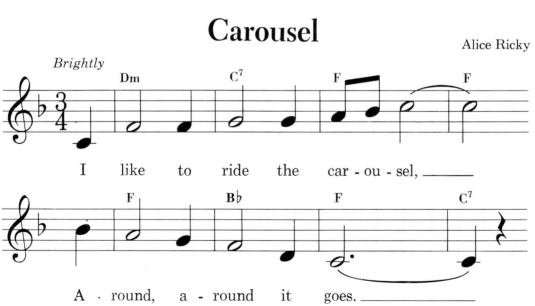

Brightly

| Dm | C⁷ | F | F |

I like to ride the car - ou - sel, _____

| F | B♭ | F | C⁷ |

A · round, a - round it goes. _____

I hear the mu - sic play - ing____

A tune that ev - 'ry - one knows.____

My moth - er and my fa - ther,____

They smile and wave good - bye.____

I like to ride the car - ou - sel____

And see the world__ go by.____

Four in a Boat

Allegro

Singing Game

1. Four in a boat and the tide rolls high,
Four in a boat and the tide rolls high,
Get you a pret - ty one bye and bye,
Get you a pret - ty one bye and bye.

2. Get me a pretty one, stay all day, . . .
We never care what the others say, . . .

3. Eight in a boat and it won't go round, . . .
Swing that pretty one you've just found, . . .

Four boys form a circle facing out, hands joined.
All others form an outer circle facing center, hands joined.
Stanza 1. Outer circle skips or walks to the left. Inner circle moves in the opposite direction.
Stanza 2. All drop hands and both circles move in the same direction. Each boy from the center chooses a girl and walks beside her.
Stanza 3. Boys from the center bring partners into the inner circle. All eight join hands and circle. Outer circle joins hands and moves in the opposite direction. At "Swing that pretty one," each boy in the inner circle swings his partner. At the end of the song he leaves her in the center. The song is repeated with the four girls in the center.

When the Village Folk Are Gay

English Version by
Helen Taylor

Latin-American Folk Song

1. I will play the vi - o - lin

When the vil - lage folk are danc - ing.

I will play the vi - o - lin

When the vil - lage folk are gay.

1-3. This way and that, I will play my vi - o - lin, oh,

This way and that, I will play my vi - o - lin.

2. I will play the clarinet, . . .   3. I will play the tambourine, . . .

Play imaginary instruments as you sing, "This way and that, . . ."

The Water Wheel

English Version by
Katherine S. Bolt

German Folk Song

1. The wa-ter wheel sings to him-self as he turns, "Crick-crack."
2. "The wheat that I grind will be made in-to bread, Crick-crack.

All cir-cled a-round with sweet flow-ers and ferns, "Crick-crack."
And all of the folk here-a-bout will be fed, Crick-crack.

"The mil-ler will bring me his wheat to be ground.
So though I may rat-tle and creak as I go,

He'll know that I'm work-ing when he hears this sound:
I'm do-ing my job in the best way I know:

Crick - crack, crick-crack, crick - crack."
Crick - crack, crick-crack, crick - crack."

Pretend that you are a large water wheel turning and turning.

Where do you find repeated tones in the melody?

Which two phrases of the melody are exactly the same?

164

DANCE -A- STORY

with **ANNE LIEF BARLIN**...about

Balloons

Written by **PAUL** and **ANNE BARLIN**
Illustrations by **LOIS ZENER THOMAS**

What is your favorite color? Is it a color like orange, that makes you feel happy and bouncy? Is it a color like soft blue, that makes you feel quiet and dreamy? Or is it a strong color like black or purple? Each color makes you feel different. When you move to the "color music" see if your body wants to move smoothly and softly — or if it wants to bounce and jump with lots of pep! Or maybe it wants to be very angry — stamping and kicking and rounding your back, like an angry cat! After you move to the music, try to guess the color you were dancing.

When you "make a magic" and turn yourself into a balloon, remember the color of your balloon. Listen to the music and feel what color the music is playing.

Would you really like to float way up in the sky? Listen to "Dance-A-Story about Balloons." Pretend real hard and the music will carry you right up to the clouds!

Anne Lief Barlin

"Dance-A-Story about Balloons," with music and narration is available on RCA Victor long-play record LE–104 and may be purchased through Ginn and Company.

What is your favorite

balloon color ?

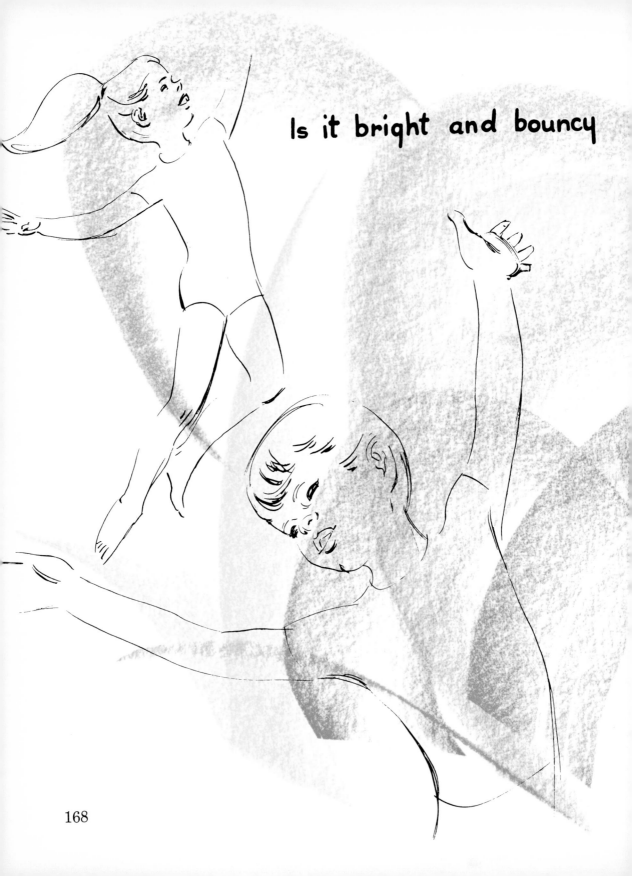

Is it bright and bouncy

...like this?

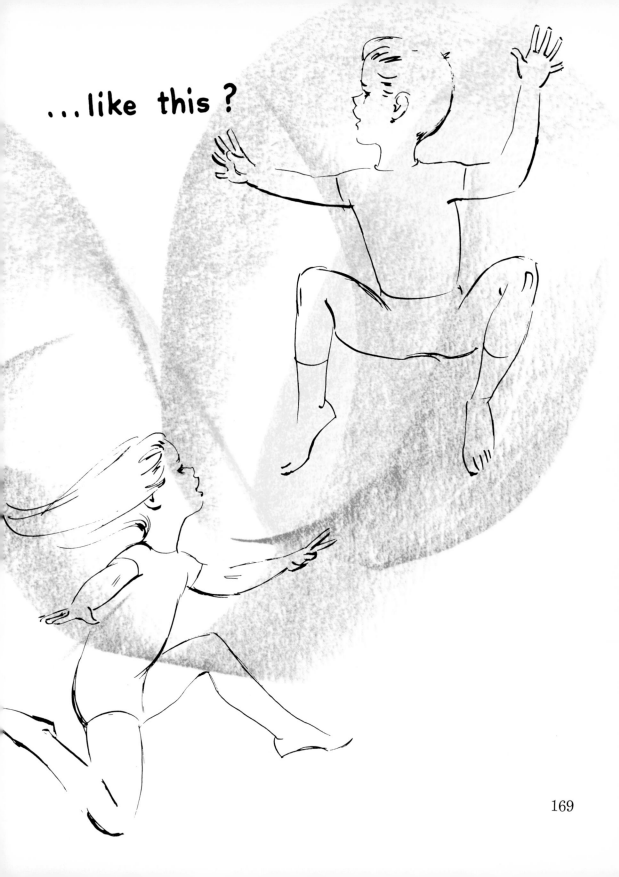

Is it light and lovely

like this?

171

Is it strong and stormy

...like this ?

Is it soft

and sad

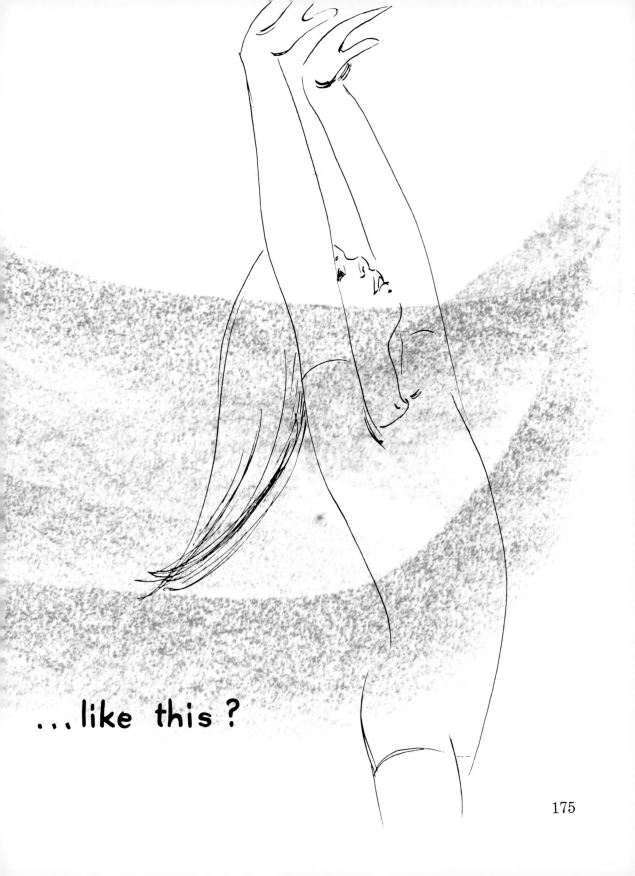

...like this?

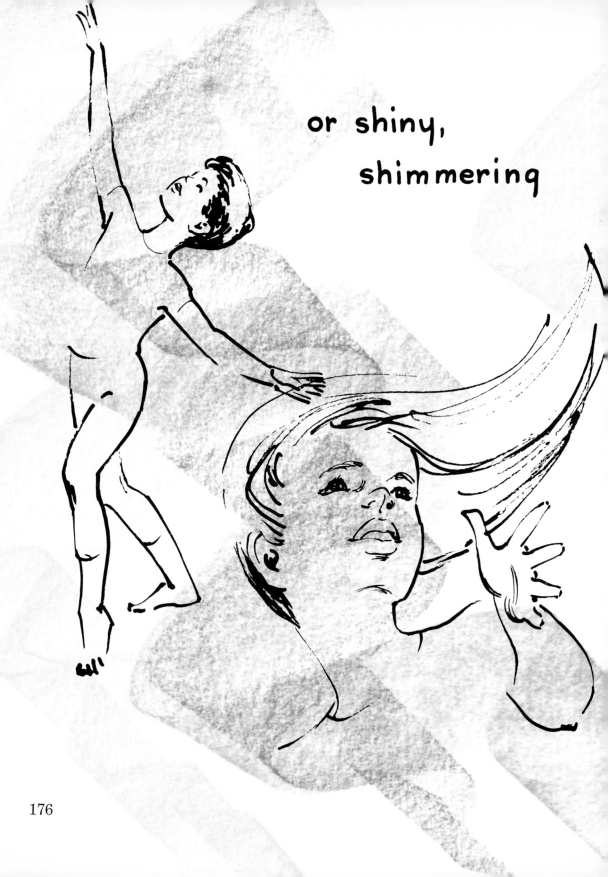

or shiny,
shimmering

...like this ?

Let's blow up a pretend
balloon. Your feet are
in "first position"

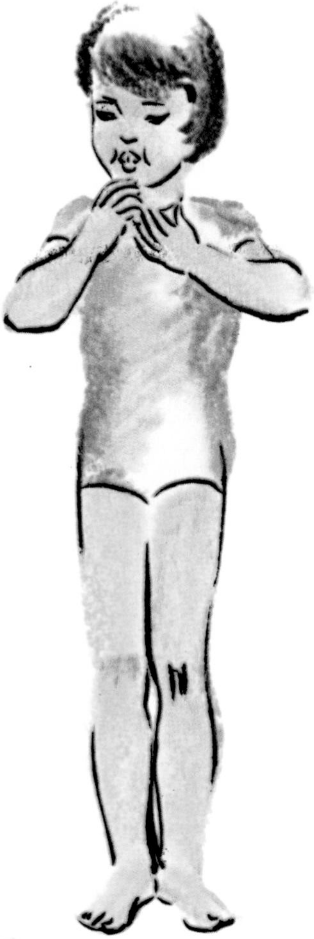

You blow

and BLOW

and BLOW

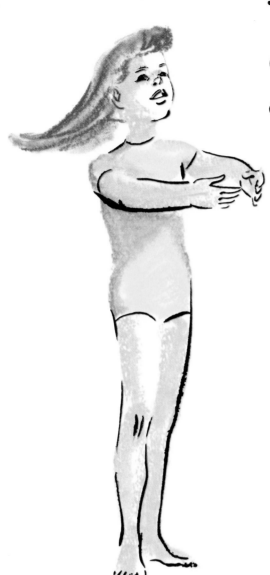

The balloon is so big
you need both arms
around it

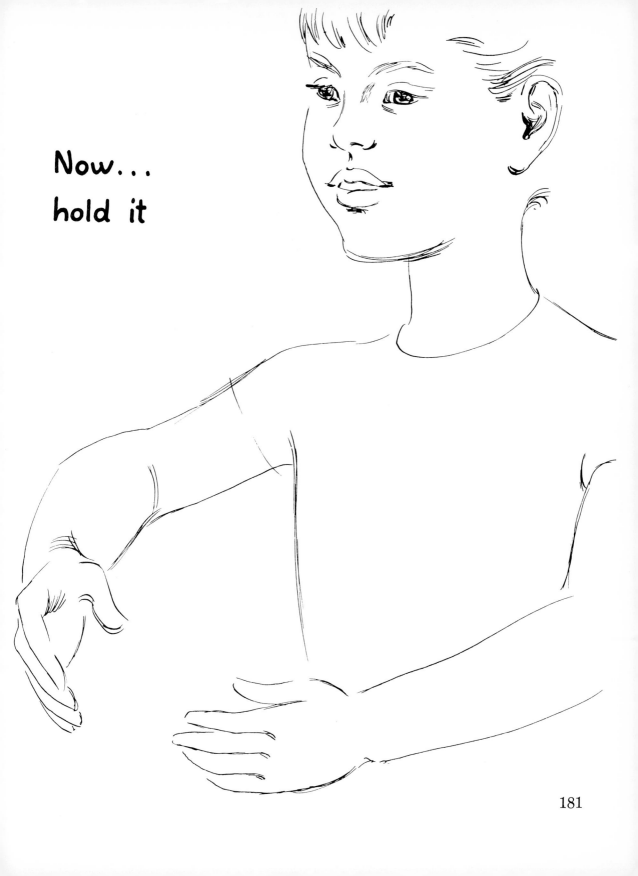

Now...
hold it

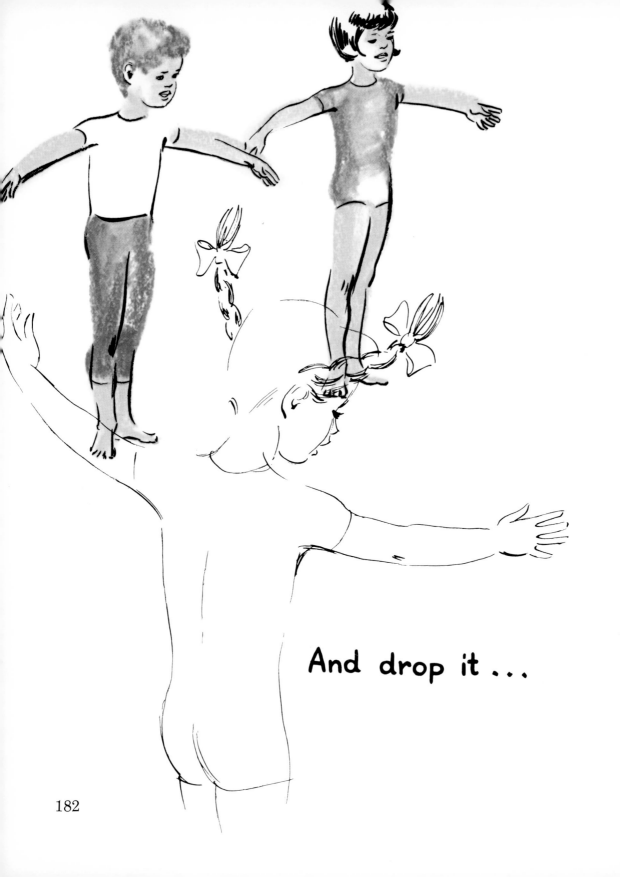

And drop it ...

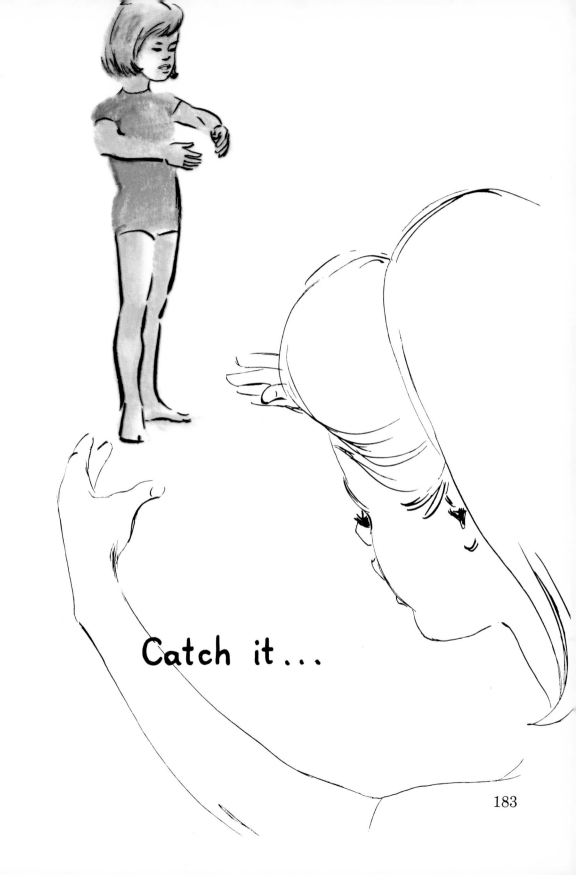

Catch it . . .

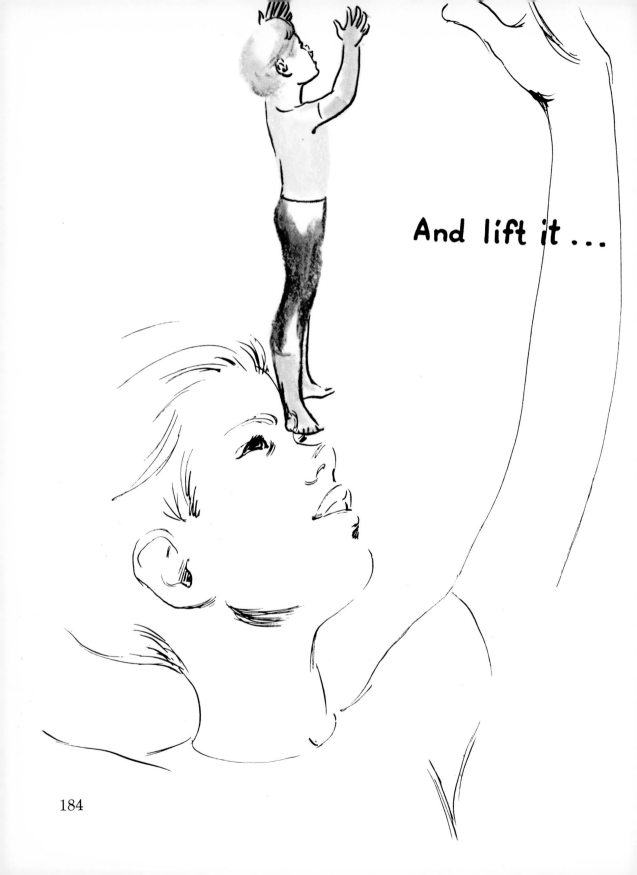

And lift it . . .

Let it go
Fly away
On tiptoe
"Relevé"

185

Away it blows
Chase it . . .

and here it is!

Throw it and catch it...

and twirl it around

"Grande Plié"
way down...

...and here it is

Let's make a magic

and turn <u>you</u>

into the balloon...

You're floating all
over the sky...

194

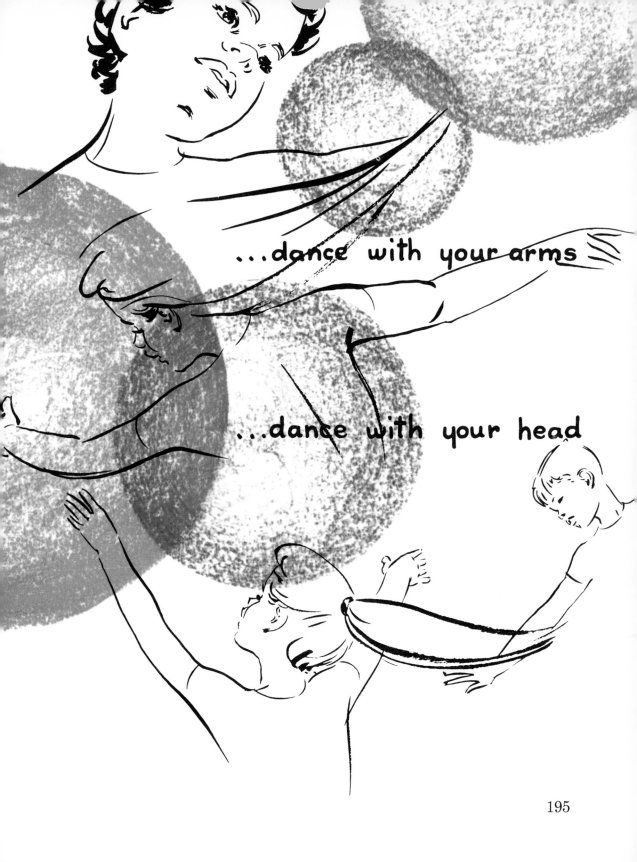

...dance with your arms

...dance with your head

The wind blows you gentl

sometimes high...

sometimes low...

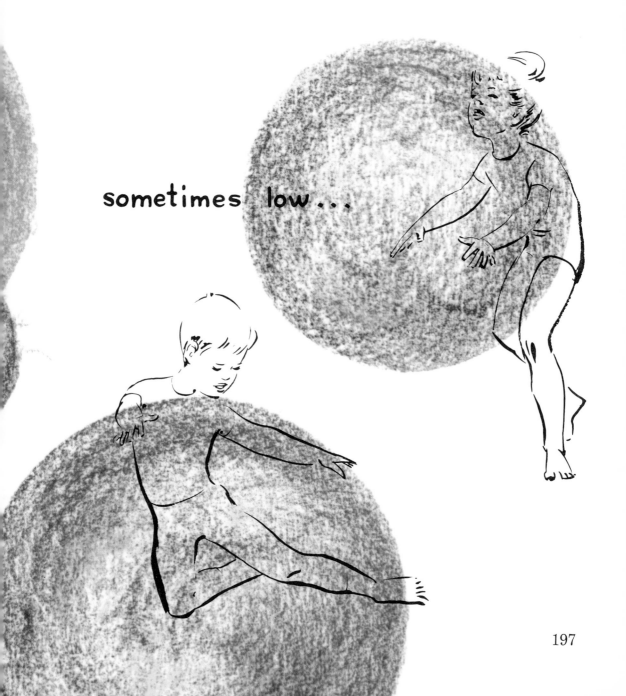

Suddenly there's a hole
in the balloon... air begins
to seep out...

You try to keep dancing

but the balloon
is getting
smaller

and

smaller...

...and

finally...

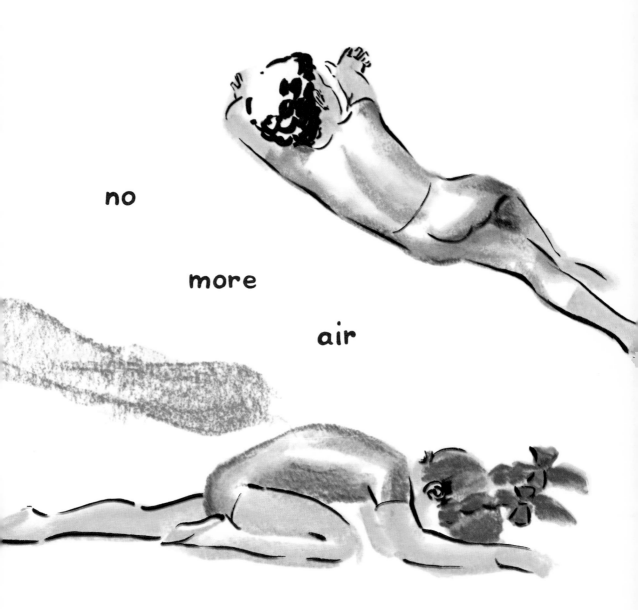

no

more

air

Let's put a patch on the balloon...

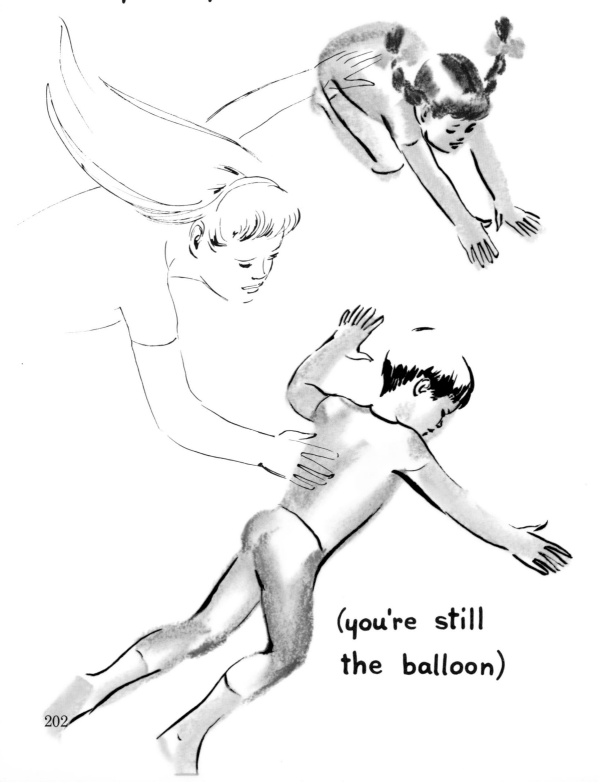

(you're still
the balloon)

202

...pretend someone is blowing you up

... you're getting bigger

and Bigger

and BIGGER

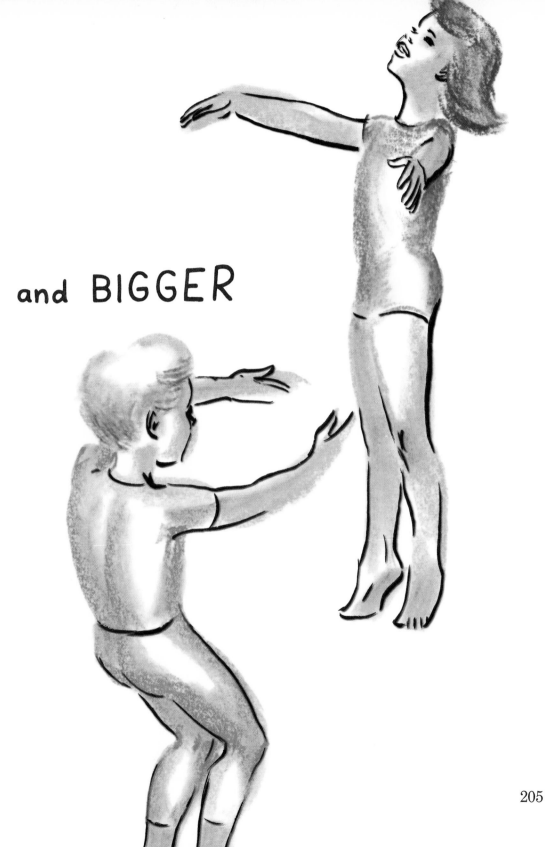

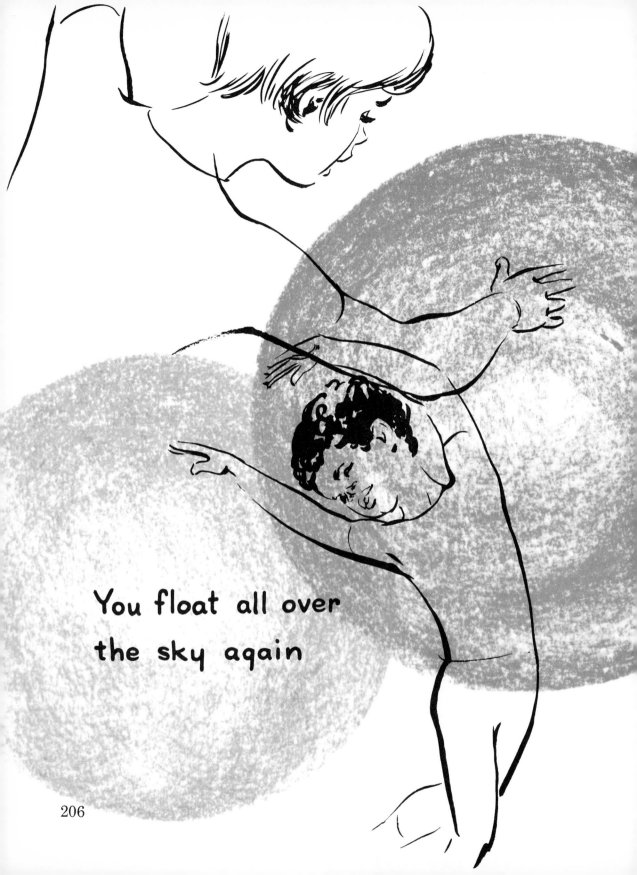

You float all over
the sky again

...dance with your head

...dance with your arms

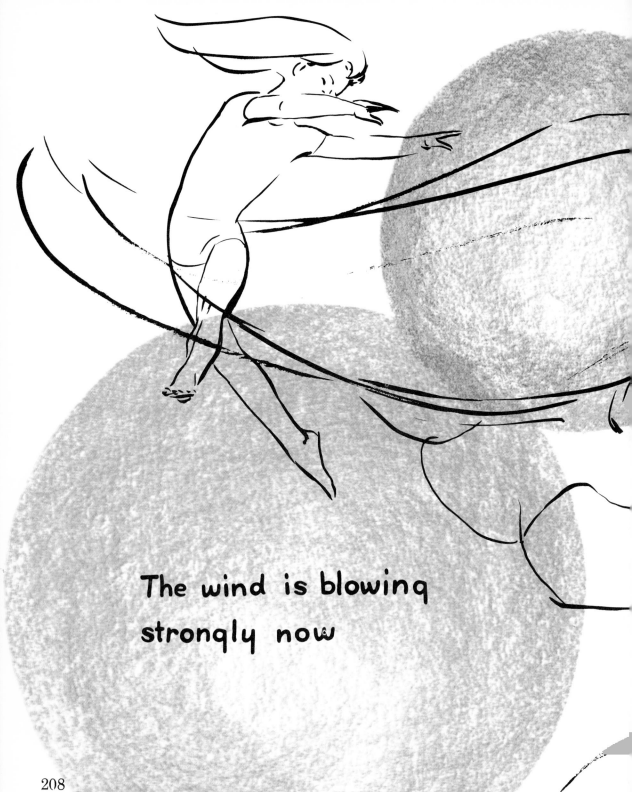

The wind is blowing
stronqly now

208

...it's getting stronger

...and STRONGER!

you're dancing
faster...

...and faster

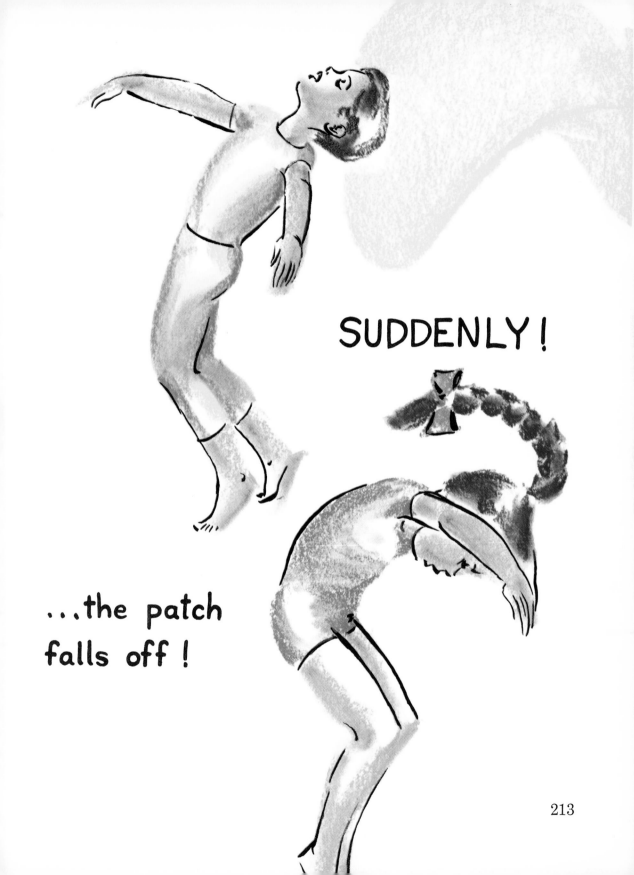

SUDDENLY!

...the patch
falls off !

213

... no

more

air.

Classified Index

My Music Dictionary

Accent: the force or "push" which makes a beat, word, or tone stronger or louder than others; > (pages 19 and 35)

Arco (*ahr'-koh*): with the bow (56)

Beat: the pulse that you feel when singing, playing, or listening to music; the sound of the bass drum in a parade or of soldiers marching; the tick of the metronome (18)

Choir: a group of singers or instrumentalists (16)

Chord: three or more tones sounded at the same time (90)

D.C. al Fine (*Da Capo al Fine*, pronounced *dah kah'-poh ahl fee'-nay*): go back to the beginning and continue to the word *Fine*, where the music ends (28)

Dotted note: the dot increases the duration of a note by one-half (31)

Duet: any two singers or instrumentalists performing together (16); also, a musical composition written for two performers

Dynamics: markings which help give expressive meaning to the music; how loudly or how softly the music is to be sung or played

pp *pianissimo* (*peeah-nees'-see-moh*): very soft (48)

p *piano* (*peeah'-noh*): soft (43)

mp *mezzo piano* (*mehd'-zoh peeah'-noh*): medium soft (41)

mf *mezzo forte* (*mehd'-zoh fohr'-tay*): medium loud (41)

f *forte* (*fohr'-tay*): loud (45)

ff *fortissimo* (*fohr-tees'-see-moh*): very loud

dim. *diminuendo* (*dee-mee-noo-ehn'-doh*): gradually softer; ▷ (43)

cresc. *crescendo* (*kray-shehn'-doh*): gradually louder; ◁ (43)

decresc. *decrescendo* (*day-kray-shehn'-doh*): gradually softer; ▷ (43)

Fermata (*fayr-mah'-tah*): a sign, often called a "hold," which makes the duration of a tone a little longer than it would be without the sign; ⌒ (85)

Fine (*fee'-nay*): the end (28)

Flat: a sign that lowers the pitch of a tone a half step; ♭ (30)

Hold: ⌒ see *Fermata*

Home tone: 1, or *do*, in a major key; the tonal center, or keynote, of a musical composition (22)

Ledger line: a short line added below (or above) the staff (26)

Legato (*lay-gah'-toh*): smooth and flowing (91)

Major scale: a series of eight tones, all going up or all going down, with a definite distance between each, the eighth tone being an octave from the first, *do-re-mi-fa-so-la-ti-do* (26)

Measure: the space between two bar lines (25)

Meter: beats grouped into sets and then into measures; some signs which stand for this grouping are $\frac{2}{4}$, $\frac{3}{4}$, $\frac{4}{4}$, $\frac{6}{8}$, C, and ¢ (19, 112)

Metronome: a device that can indicate by a ticking sound the tempo or speed of music in an exact number of beats per minute (21)

Notes: signs that stand for the duration of sound; different kinds of notes tell how long to sing or play tones; placed on a staff with a clef, notes stand for both the duration and pitch of sounds; see also *Rests*

    o   whole note (22)

    ♩. dotted half note (23)

    ♩ half note (22)

    ♩. dotted quarter note (31)

    ♩ quarter note (22)

    ♫, ♪ ♪ eighth notes (25)

    ♬, ♬♬ sixteenth notes (141)

Octave: the distance between one tone and the next higher or lower tone having the same letter name

Pattern: a short musical idea which is repeated

Phrase: in music, a series of tones, often four measures long, which expresses a musical idea (30)

Pizzicato (*peet-see-kah'-toh*): plucked or picked (56)

Quartet: any four singers or instrumentalists performing together; also, a musical composition written for four performers (16)

Repeat signs: signs that tell what part of the music is to be sung or played once again; one repeat sign means to go back to the beginning and sing or play the music again, :‖ (83); two repeat signs mean to play the music in between them once more, ‖: :‖ (83); see also *D.C. al Fine*

Rests: signs that stand for the duration of silence; different kinds of rests tell how long to be silent; see also *Notes*

    ▬ whole rest (118)

    ▬ half rest (64)

    𝄽 quarter rest (64)

    𝄾 eighth rest (51)

    𝄿 sixteenth rest

Round: a song that can be sung over and over by two or more voices, the voices entering at regular periods, starting on the same tone, as in the popular round "Lovely Evening" (90)

Sharp: a sign that raises the pitch of a tone a half step; ♯ (33)

Solo: any one singer or instrumentalist performing alone or with accompaniment; also, a musical composition written for one performer (16)

220

Staff: the five lines and four spaces upon which notes and other signs of music are written (26)

Symphony: a composition for orchestra that usually has three or more separate movements, although some have only one or two (19); also, the name given to an orchestra that plays symphonic music (54)

Tempo: the speed at which music is sung or played; the speed of the beat

ritard. *ritardando* (*ree-tahr-dahn′-doh*): gradually slower (43)

a tempo (*ah tehm′-poh*): return to the same speed as before (43)

See also page 21

Theme: an important melody of a musical composition (109)

Tone: a sound of definite pitch (22)

Treble clef: a sign that determines the pitch and names for the lines and spaces of the staff; often called "G clef" because it circles around the second line of the staff and gives to that line the name G (26)

Trio: any three singers or instrumentalists performing together; also, a composition written for three performers (16)

Alphabetical Index

All selections are recorded in Albums MM–3A, MM–3B, MM–3C, and MM–3D as designated.

"Dance-A-Story about Balloons," with music and narration, is available on RCA Victor long-play record LE–104 and may be purchased through Ginn and Company.

Index of First Lines of Poems

GH–0765

PRINTED IN THE UNITED STATES OF AMERICA

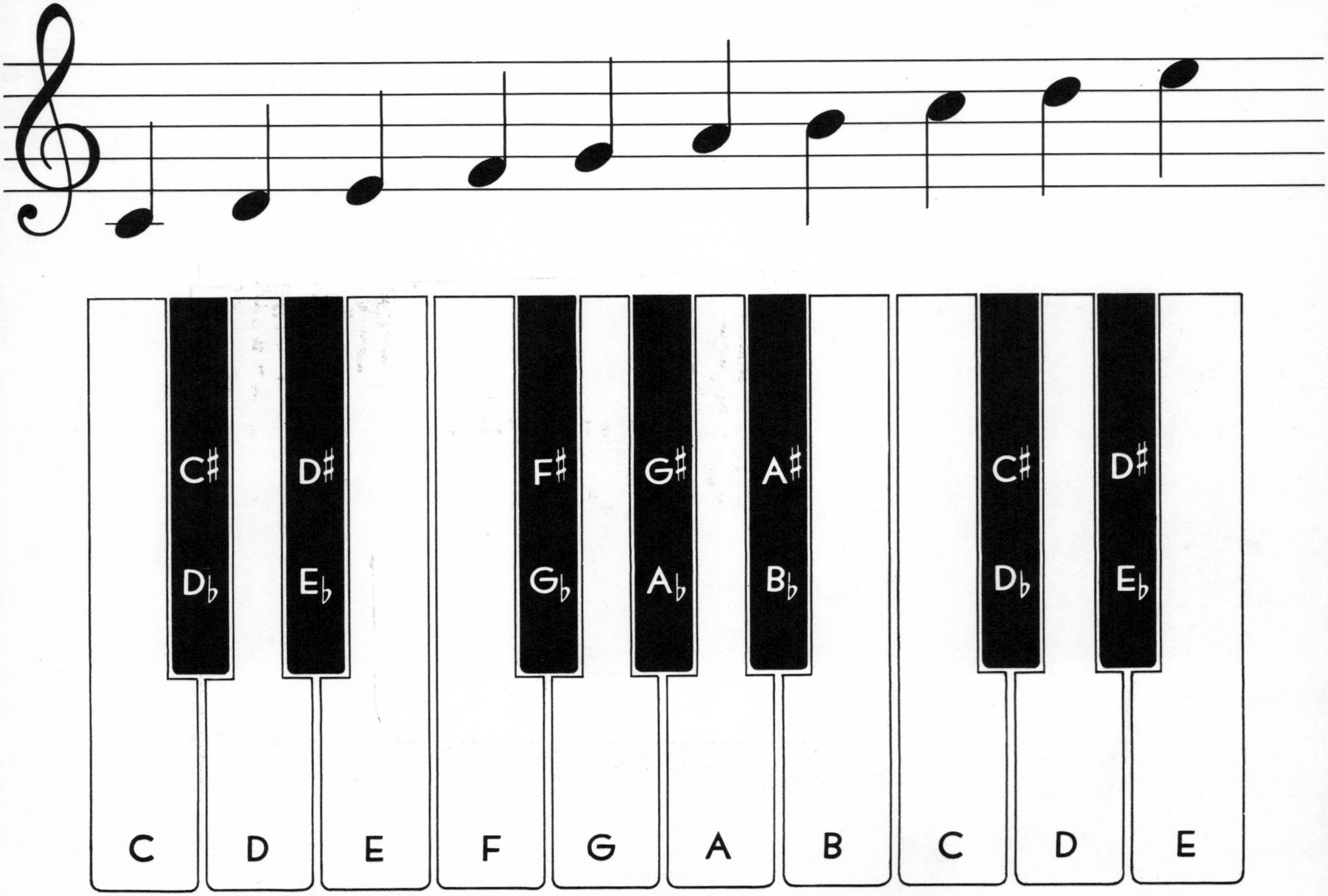

D71000335782